# EARLY CHRISTIAN LATIN POETS

This is the first substantial overview of the Golden Age of Christian Latin poetry, from the fourth to sixth centuries. The poets studied range from familiar names such as Ambrose, Augustine and Prudentius, to lesser-known figures such as Arator, Dracontius and Avitus. Their work was hugely influential on English and French medieval literature, but has often been disregarded by critics as a pale imitation of the great names of the classical past.

Carolinne White's illuminating study sets the works in their literary and historical context, and shows how these poets were motivated by a desire to convey the truth of the Christian message. Questions of form and content, continuity with classical culture, theological issues and contemporary heresies are all explored, prior to clear, sensitive translations of over thirty poems and excerpts, many of which have never before been translated into English.

This useful volume fully conveys the true importance of the early Christian Latin poets, and makes their work accessible to a wider audience than ever before.

**Carolinne White** is a tutor in medieval Latin, and a lexicographer on the *Medieval Latin Dictionary* at the University of Oxford. Her previous publications include *Early Christian Lives* (1998).

# THE EARLY CHURCH FATHERS
Edited by Carol Harrison
*University of Durham*

The Greek and Latin Fathers of the Church are central to the creation of Christian doctrine, yet often unapproachable because of the sheer volume of their writings and the relative paucity of accessible translations. This series makes available translations of key selected texts by the major Fathers to all students of the early Church.

*Already published:*
## MAXIMUS THE CONFESSOR
*Andrew Louth*

## IRENAEUS OF LYONS
*Robert M. Grant*

## AMBROSE
*Boniface Ramsey, OP*

## ORIGEN
*Joseph W. Trigg*

## GREGORY OF NYSSA
*Anthony Meredith, SJ*

## JOHN CHRYSOSTOM
*Wendy Mayer and Pauline Allen*

## CYRIL OF ALEXANDRIA
*Norman Russell*

## CYRIL OF JERUSALEM
*Edward Yarnold, SJ*

# EARLY CHRISTIAN LATIN POETS

*Carolinne White*

London and New York

First published 2000
by Routledge
11 New Fetter Lane, London EC4P 4EE

Simultaneously published in the USA and Canada
by Routledge
29 West 35th Street, New York, NY 10001

*Routledge is an imprint of the Taylor & Francis Group*

Typeset in Garamond by
M Rules
Printed and bound in Great Britain by
TJ International Ltd, Padstow, Cornwall

*British Library Cataloguing in Publication Data*
A catalogue record for this book is available from the British Library

*Library of Congress Cataloguing in Publication Data*
White, Caroline
Early Christian Latin poets/Carolinne White.
p.cm. – (The early church fathers)
Includes bibliographical references and index.
1. Christian poetry, Latin – History and criticism.
2. Christianity and literature – Rome.
I. Title. II. Series.

PA6053.W47 2000
871′.01099222–dc21                                              00-038244

ISBN 0–415–18782–6 (hbk)
ISBN 0–415–18783–4 (pbk)

# CONTENTS

# CONTENTS

# ABBREVIATIONS

ACW        *Ancient Christian Writers*, Newman Press, 1946ff.
CCSL       *Corpus Christianorum*, Series Latina, Turnhout, 1953ff.
CSEL       *Corpus Scriptorum Ecclesiasticorum Latinorum*, Vienna, 1866ff.
FC         *Fathers of the Church*, Washington, DC: The Catholic University of America Press, 1947ff.
MGH AA     *Monumenta Germaniae Historica, Auctores Antiquissimi*, Berlin, 1877ff.
PL         J.-P. Migne (ed.), *Patrologia Latina*, Paris, 1841ff.
SC         *Sources Chrétiennes*, Paris: Cerf, 1941ff.

# PREFACE

The poems and excerpts from poems included in this anthology have been chosen from the large corpus of early Christian Latin poetry to give an idea of the range of subjects treated by poets in the period 300–600 CE whose motivation to write poetry came from their Christian faith. Most of the extant poems from this period are lengthy – too long to be included here in their entirety – but where possible I have translated complete poems. Reference to the editions of the Latin texts is made in the brief introductions to each poet or anonymous poem, while the select bibliography provides information on secondary literature to enable the reader to explore the texts and subjects further.

With regard to the translations, I am well aware of the truth of Bede's words: 'It is not possible to translate verse, however well composed, literally from one language to another without some loss of beauty and dignity.' I have taken a middle course between reducing the poetry to prose and producing a metrical translation: these translations follow the original more or less line by line but no attempt is made to imitate the original metres as this, I believe, would sound more stilted to the contemporary English reader than the Latin verse did to the readers of Late Antiquity. My concern has been to provide as clear and accurate a translation as possible so that the reader may gain an understanding of the content of these poems; some idea of the form of the original can be gained from the brief information given in the individual introductions. In putting content before form, I follow the reasoning of Erasmus who wrote, 'Speech consists of two parts – of words comparable to the body, and meaning comparable to the soul. If both can be rendered I have no objection to it being done. If this is not possible, it would be wrong for a translator to keep to the words and deviate from the meaning.'

Carolinne White

# Part 1

# INTRODUCTION

# BACKGROUND TO
# THE TEXTS

The long neglect of early Christian Latin poetry (which is usually taken to consist of poems by authors from Italy, Gaul, Spain and North Africa in the period from the early fourth century to the late sixth century) perhaps arises from the attitudes of Renaissance humanists who considered medieval literature as inferior to the extant works of such writers as Cicero, Horace and Virgil who were writing in the relatively short period of history that came to be termed 'classical antiquity'. Vives denounced the poetry of Juvencus, Sedulius, Prosper and Paulinus as muddy waters[1] and Aldus Manutius claimed that 'among the learned of Italy he had met not one who had read a line of ancient Christian poetry'. And yet Petrarch admired Lactantius and Augustine for combining the 'studia humanitatis' with the 'studia divinitatis', and spoke approvingly of Arator, Prudentius, Sedulius and Juvencus in his tenth Eclogue; Luther called Sedulius 'the most Christian poet'[2] and John Colet recommended the reading of Lactantius, Juvencus, Proba, Prudentius and Sedulius, as writers of 'clean and chaste Latin' like that used by Cicero, Sallust, Virgil and Terence.[3] But if during the Renaissance and Reformation the new enthusiasm for the writers of classical antiquity was often combined with an understanding of the importance of the Christian writers of late antiquity, the rather negative view of medieval 'Dark Age' civilization was reinforced during the so-called Enlightenment with its suspicion of the Catholic Church. The study of the Christian poets of late antiquity has suffered as a result of this suspicion. Classicists have apparently been put off by the Christian content and theologians by the poetic form. The tendency has been to drive a wedge between the classical and the Christian, denying any continuity between them[4] and thereby also denying any quality to the Christian product. Even if we admit the superiority of some of the classical poets, it is nevertheless true that early Christian Latin poetry deserves attention for its

3

content and not merely for any formal and stylistic similarities it bears to classical poetry. It is a poetry that covers a wide variety of subjects and forms – theological points and doctrinal issues, anti-pagan and anti-heretical polemic, moral advice, saints' lives and miracles, hymns, biblical epic based on both the Old Testament and the New, and pastoral, as well as more personal lyric, epigrams, consolation in bereavement and autobiographical poetry. It is a poetry in which these themes are often treated with imaginative richness, allowing the reader to perceive a spiritual meaning as well as the literal.[5] It is a poetry in which the Latin language develops beyond the boundaries set by classical literary Latin, using new terms associated with Christianity and often derived from Vulgar Latin,[6] but also using classical words in new ways. It is a poetry in which the poet's passionate commitment to Christianity is often evident and which is not merely the product of a leisured elite. And finally, many of these poems came to be regarded by medieval readers as classics in their own right, becoming part of the school curriculum and having a strong influence on the creation of medieval literature in Latin and the vernacular languages.

However, despite a general wariness with regard to this body of literature, the last two decades have seen a growth in the number of critical studies devoted to it, the principal areas of study being the works of Prudentius and Paulinus of Nola, who have long been regarded as the Christian poets *par excellence*, and the genre of biblical epic, covering the work of Juvencus from the early fourth century, through that of Proba, Sedulius, Cyprian the Poet (also known as Cyprian of Gaul), Claudius Marius Victorius, and Avitus, down to Arator's verse commentary on the Acts of the Apostles in 544. Nevertheless, there remains much that is controversial and much work remains to be done in establishing decent editions of early Christian poems, in discussing their style, content, historical setting and the influence on them of the growing body of biblical exegesis, as well as in introducing the less well-known poems to a wider audience.

It may seem surprising that the term 'early Christian Latin poetry' is used to cover the poetry produced in the period from the early fourth century when, under the Emperor Constantine, Christianity first became a tolerated religion within the Roman Empire, until the late sixth century. Why do we not have any Latin poems on Christian themes dating from the first three centuries of the Christian era? Although we can give no precise answers, a number of points are relevant here. It may of course be that poems from that period have been lost,[7] but it would seem that until the middle of the third century or the beginning of the fourth, the language of the Church even in the West was Greek rather than Latin;[8] the liturgy of the early Church was heavily influenced by Jewish and Hellenistic sources, less so by the culture of the Latin-speaking West. Although there seems to have existed a flourishing Christian hymnody alongside the use of the psalms, these were hymns in Greek and Syriac,[9] rather than in Latin: it was not until the work of Hilary of Poitiers and Ambrose in the fourth century that a specifically Latin hymnody developed. Before this time, Christians, living with the threat of persecution by the authorities, tended to be suspicious of pagan culture and the kind of poetry it produced. In contrast, the period from the fourth to the sixth century was a time of prodigious intellectual activity which saw advances in book production, in work on the biblical text and revision of its translation into Latin from Greek and Hebrew, and in biblical study which resulted in many works of exegesis explaining the meaning of Scripture.

Furthermore, it was not before the momentous events of the early fourth century that the Church gradually gained in strength and self-confidence, as Christians were no longer subject to persecution by the state authorities and as increasing numbers of educated people decided, for whatever reason, to convert from paganism to Christianity: these factors may well have affected the type of poetry produced when Latin Christianity found its poetic voice.

For despite the fact that the poetry with which most Christians in the early centuries would have come into contact in their lives as Christians would have been the psalms of the Old Testament,[10] chanted or sung during the performance of the liturgy – Tertullian, for example, mentions the chanting of psalms alongside the reading of the scriptures, the preaching of sermons and the offering up of prayers as essential components of the liturgy[11] – the earliest Christian Latin poetry that has come down to us is no mere imitation of the Hebrew psalms, with their characteristic parallelisms, word pairings, and direct address from the human poet to the divine creator. Only in the occasional use of the abecedarian form in which each stanza or section starts with a letter in alphabetical sequence, as in two of the fragmentary hymns of Hilary of Poitiers, Augustine's *Psalm against the Donatists*, and in Sedulius's hymn *A solis ortus cardine*, do we find something that is likely to derive from Semitic poetry: perhaps the most famous example of an abecedarian poem is Psalm 119. With regard to liturgical literature, it is true that a few works of Christian poetry were designed for use in the liturgy or at the shrines of martyrs, works such as the hymns of Hilary of Poitiers or of Ambrose, the abecedarian psalm against the Donatists of Augustine, even perhaps sections of Prudentius' *Cathemerinon* (*The Daily Round*) and *Peristephanon* (*The Martyrs' Crowns*). Despite the largely theological and biblical content of Christian Latin poetry, its form, style and aesthetics arguably owe far more to pagan Latin poetry, particularly Virgil, but also to Horace, Ovid, Statius and Lucan.[12] Not only do early Christian Latin poets use hexameters and other quantitative metres employed by the aforesaid poets but they pluck lines and phrases from these poets,[13] though setting them in a new Christian context which alters and even negates the original meaning.[14]

It would therefore be misleading to think that the early Christian poets were aiming to create a body of liturgical literature in Latin but equally misleading to suggest that they were merely creating belletristic works with a Christian content to replace the standard pagan authors. The latter was admittedly attempted in the Greek-speaking world by Bishop Apollinaris of Laodicea and his son, following the Emperor Julian's edict in 362 forbidding Christians to teach Greek literature: according to the historian Socrates, they paraphrased Scripture in the form of Greek epic, tragedy, comedy and lyric, so that Christians might yet learn about the Greek literary forms. On the whole, it would be more correct to see the purpose of early Christian Latin poetry as stemming from the desire of Christians who happened to be more or less well versed in classical literature to communicate the truth of the Christian message, to argue against pagan and heretical views and to praise God outside the liturgical context. In the words of Charlet, 'poetic activity became a spiritual act, a form of divine worship and the poem itself an offering to God.'[15]

It was in fact the content of the poems, the expression of what was regarded as the truth, that was important, while the form of the poems was considered as secondary, a way of making the content more beautiful and persuasive.[16] Poetry was not just a way of dressing up a pleasant or amusing idea but a means of packaging the crucial message of Christianity regarding human salvation in the most effective and appropriate manner. In holding the view that the classical forms and metres in fact offered the best packaging, the poets manifested the influence of their education, for anyone who was regarded as educated would have been trained in grammar and rhetoric by means of close study and imitation of such writers as Virgil, Horace and Ovid. Even such luminaries of the Church as Augustine, Ambrose, Basil and Gregory of Nazianzus whose parents were Christian were all given a traditional education. Given such familiarity with the earlier poets, it was natural even for Christian poets to express themselves in similar styles. Even when Paulinus of Nola, now that he has committed himself to Christ, rejects the literary and aesthetic ideals of his mentor Ausonius, it is not the classical forms that he spurns, but the pagan themes and a view of poetry as something essentially lightweight, a form of amusement rather than a vehicle for serious truth. Both the *Cento Nuptialis* of Ausonius, whose sympathies lay with pagan thought, and the *Cento* of the Christian lady Proba consist of a patchwork of Virgilian lines. And yet Ausonius regards his own as a frivolous work while Proba claims to be attempting to bring Virgil onto a higher plane by using him to convey the truth of salvation history, to persuade people to read the Bible and to live in a Christian fashion.

Alongside the influence of the education system, we can see that the generally more favourable attitude to rhetoric and poetry in the fourth century may also have helped to encourage the writing of Christian poetry. If Tertullian at the beginning of the third century had a fundamentally negative attitude to secular learning[17] while admitting that some contact with it was regrettably necessary as a basis for Christian studies, by the fourth century there was room for a more ambivalent attitude. Although eloquence is not necessary for the expression of the truth, it can help to make the truth more palatable and to reach a wider audience. As Lactantius writes:

> Although the truth may be defended without eloquence, as it often has been defended by many, yet it needs to be explained and in a measure discussed, with distinctness and elegance of speech, in order that it may flow with greater power into the minds of men;[18]

while almost a century later Paulinus of Nola advises a friend on the use of pagan rhetoric, writing to him:

> Let it be enough for you to have taken from them your fluency of speech and verbal adornment like spoils taken from enemy arms, so that stripped of their errors and clothed in their eloquence you may adapt to the fulness of reality the sheen of eloquence used by empty wisdom to deceive. Thus you may adorn not the empty body of unreality but the full body of truth and ponder thoughts which are not merely pleasing to human ears but also of benefit to human minds.[19]

The fact that so much of Christian poetry is created in the image of the pagan poets may also be due to the difficulties which many cultured Christians of the fourth century had with the style of the Scriptures.[20] We know, for example, that both Augustine and Jerome found the style rebarbative at first, though gradually familiarity with it bred admiration. By the time Ambrose composed his hymns in the 380s he clearly felt happy with a form of poetry more akin to the apparently unsophisticated style of the Bible, though he still chose to write these verses in a traditional, if simple, metre. Jerome, writing a letter to Paulinus of Nola in 394, gives the following advice:

> Let not the simplicity of scripture or the poverty of its vocabulary offend you, for these are due either to the faults of translators or else to a deliberate purpose, for in this way it is better fitted for the instruction of an unlettered congregation as the educated person can take one meaning and the uneducated another from one and the same sentence.[21]

But why did Christians feel impelled to write poetry rather than prose, considering that Latin poetry had hitherto carried a certain stigma in the eyes of Christians because of the immoral, fictional subjects it treated which were deemed to distract from the study of the sacred writings and even to incite readers to immoral behaviour?[22] Certainly, Christians were not supposed to compose poetry on non-Christian subjects: Augustine, for example, criticizes the young man Licentius for writing such poetry rather than focusing on Christ, and advises him to visit Paulinus at Nola to learn how to lead a truly Christian life.[23] But it was not only the content that was problematic; it was also the seductive quality of the beauty of the verse forms which was regarded as dangerous and more likely to enable the mendacities of the pagan world-view to infiltrate the soul.[24]

However, Christians could see that poetic form, like the use of rhetoric, could be used to embellish and convey the truth as well as falsehood. While they condemn in no uncertain terms the fictions which they see in pagan poetry, they do – perhaps surprisingly – hold the view that it is possible to use the forms of pagan poetry to express the truths of biblical revelation. In regarding pagan poetry as containing lies, Christians were continuing a tradition of literary criticism which went back to the earliest Greek poets and philosophers. Had not Hesiod shown that he was aware of the problem of poetic truth when he puts the following words in the mouth of the Muses: 'We know how to speak many false things, as though they were true, but we know how to utter true things if we want to'?[25] Had not Xenophanes attacked the portrayal of the gods by Homer and Hesiod and rejected poetry about giants and centaurs as fiction?[26] If most critics in classical antiquity would have admitted that poetry contained much that was not true, they found different ways of dealing with this fact. One way was to remove any moral criteria and to claim, as the Sophists in classical Athens had done, that since poetry is written with a view to pleasure rather than truth, what is to be admired in a poet is his ability to create something plausible and attractive. Aristotle believed that the correctness of poetry is not a matter of ethics but of the accuracy with which the poet represents what he set out to represent.[27] Plutarch, in his essay on *How the young man should study poetry*, cannot disregard the ethical question but while admitting that poetry contained much that was disturbing and misleading, he believed that if the reader was trained to admire virtue and combined the study of poetry with that of philosophy, then the poetry would not affect him adversely. Another way of dealing with the problem was to say that the poems meant something different from their literal meaning. This tended to be the view held by the educators, those whose aim was to instruct and give moral guidance. Here were the beginnings of allegorical interpretation, a method which was later to flourish for many centuries within Christian culture when it was used to explain the meaning of the Scriptures,[28] though it is interesting that Christians on the whole did not attempt to allegorize the content of pagan poetry at this early stage.[29]

On the face of it, Plato's rejection of the poets might appear to have much in common with the suspicion with which Christians regarded them; indeed, Augustine praises Plato for ejecting the poets from his ideal state to prevent them misleading the citizens.[30] Plato seems to have rejected all poetry except hymns and praises poetry on the grounds that it strengthens the irrational elements of the soul and deals with appearances rather than with reality.[31] Given such criticisms from within classical culture it would not have been surprising if Christians had adopted the view that poetry was dangerous and that the writing of it should be avoided at all costs even if they believed that the truth, equated with the Christian gospel and essential to man's happiness and salvation, could and should be communicated by means of language and rhetoric.

So, how did they justify the use of poetry rather than prose to convey the truth? First of all, they saw that poetic forms had been used in the Old Testament, not only in the Psalms[32] but also in the Books of Job, Jeremiah and the Song of Songs. They believed that

Hebrew poetry was earlier than pagan poetry and that in some sense it provided a viable alternative to pagan poetry: Jerome, for example, writes to Paulinus of Nola in his *Letter* 53 that 'David, who is our Simonides, Pindar and Alcaeus, our Horace, our Catullus and our Serenus all in one, sings of Christ to his lyre.' However, this does not explain why, when Christians came to write poetry, they mainly used poetic forms so closely associated with the literature of those who had been regarded as inimical to Christianity. We have mentioned the familiarity they had with such forms through their education and the gradual, if not wholly consistent, change in attitude to some of what secular culture had to offer.[33] There was also the view, inherited from pagan antiquity, that poetry had a powerful didactic role, and Christians were able to develop this into a view whereby the aim of poetry was doctrinal, moral and spiritual instruction.

Furthermore, they came to see that pleasure, such as that gained from a well-composed poem, was not necessarily a bad thing if it was coupled with virtue and divine truth, rather than being distorted to vice and falsehood;[34] and many educated Christians did clearly believe that pagan poetic forms offered the greatest pleasure to the reader, given that most of the poetry composed was written by the educated for the educated, notable exceptions being Ambrose's *Hymns* and Augustine's *Psalm against the Donatists* written for use by ordinary church congregations in Milan and North Africa, respectively. With regard to poetic style, it was possible to perceive a certain continuity between the Bible and the rhetorical techniques of secular literature[35] which would not only encourage those educated in secular literature to look at the biblical style more positively but might justify the use of such techniques even in a specifically Christian literature.

In this context it is illuminating to consider what the early Christian poets themselves have to say about their reasons for writing poetry, as put forward in the prefaces, prologues or dedicatory letters accompanying their compositions. Juvencus seems relatively untroubled when, in introducing his account of Christ's life based on the Gospels, he says that although nothing in this world is everlasting, poets can make virtue and great achievements live on; if Homer and Virgil can make things that are untrue live on, will it not be much more possible for the true faith to live on through poetry? Juvencus also puts a new spin on the traditional belief that poets gain lasting fame for themselves through their poetry[36] when he expresses the hope that God will reward him for his work by looking favourably on the poet at the Last Judgement. Similarly, Sedulius confidently dismisses the figments and lies of the pagan poets in favour of the truth of Christ's miracles and their significance for our understanding of God and man's salvation: why should we prefer barren land covered in weeds to a lovely green landscape? He also holds the view that poetry, being more pleasurable than prose, is better at putting its message across. Avitus, too, associates poetry with a licence to lie, but seems to think it is possible, if difficult, to express the truth poetically (in accordance with the wishes of his dedicatee), as long as form is subordinated to content and poetic licence is not used to justify saying what is not true or not in accordance with the Christian faith. At the beginning of his sixth book Avitus contrasts the trifling verse form with the important content and hopes it will bring his sister pleasure, stressing that his lyre is not tainted by falsehood, thus distancing himself from pagan influence. Some poets lay stress on the idea that the poet is a channel for conveying God's truth[37] and as such has a duty to write, inspired by Christ or the Holy Spirit rather than the Muses. Others are apparently inspired to write poetry after their conversion, in order to praise God and to make known the truth to others: Prudentius, for example, seems to think it natural to use verses to praise God, honour the martyrs and combat heresy. For him, a poem is a most suitable offering to God: 'with voice at least may my sinning soul honour God, even if with good deeds it cannot', as he writes in his Preface.

In considering these Christian poems produced during the course of several centuries, it is possible to hold both that there was a strong element of continuity between the pagan and Christian – that the Latin poetic tradition was still a living one in the fourth and following centuries – and that a break in continuity occurred as regards the poetic subject: the combination of this continuity and break in continuity together produced a poetry of great richness, for the Christian poets could not only use the polished forms of pagan poetry but revitalize these forms by means of an infusion of new subject matter and the consequent lively tension between old and new.[38]

The poems of Christian antiquity can be grouped according to theme, form or the purpose of their composition. First, there are hymns by such writers as Hilary of Poitiers, Ambrose, Prudentius, Sedulius, Ennodius and Venantius Fortunatus: these were composed in a variety of ancient metres and for a variety of occasions, both liturgical and non-liturgical, public and private devotion; nevertheless there are certain broad categories into which they can be fitted, for they were all written either for certain festivals or times of day, celebrating aspects of the triune God – especially the incarnate Christ – or the achievements of particular saints and martyrs. Occasionally verses in the form of a hymn stand at the head of a longer work, as in the case of Dracontius' *De Laudibus Dei* (*The Praises of God*).

Certain long poems in hexameters are generally considered together under the heading of biblical epic, though it should not be overlooked that they differ from one another in important ways and are by no means all paraphrases of Scripture in Virgilian verse. From this period survive the poems on Old Testament subjects – particularly on the account of the Creation and the Fall recounted in the early chapters of Genesis – by Cyprian the Poet, Claudius Marius Victorius, Avitus, together with the shorter *Metrum in Genesim* (*Poem on Genesis*) ascribed to a certain Hilary (but not Hilary of Poitiers or Hilary of Arles), while Juvencus and Sedulius chose to write on aspects of the life of Christ, and Arator on material taken from the Acts of the Apostles; the poem by the aristocratic lady Faltonia Proba, consisting exclusively of lines and half-lines taken from Virgil's poetry, covers both Old and New Testament themes. Some of the subjects treated at length in these poems, being crucial to the Christian understanding of God's dealings with mankind, also inevitably occur in other kinds of poetry. Prudentius, for example, gives a brief account of God's creation of mankind and Adam and Eve's sin in the third of the hymns in his *Cathemerinon* (96–150); the crossing of the Red Sea by the Israelites is treated not only by Cyprian the Poet, but also by Prudentius in *Cathemerinon* 5 (57–88) and by Sedulius in Book 1 of his *Carmen Paschale* (136–147). If Sedulius' main theme is the miracles of Christ, these are also summarized by Prudentius in *Cathemerinon* 9 (28–69); in both cases the miracles culminate in Christ's death and resurrection. This latter theme also occurs in Prudentius' work *Contra Symmachum* (*Against Symmachus*) (2.129–211) and in Dracontius' second book (527–561). The crucial theme of God's salvation of mankind through Christ's death on the cross, his atonement for our sins and resurrection from the dead are handled in less direct ways in Lactantius' *Phoenix* and in Endelechius' pastoral on the apparently unrelated topic of the deaths of cattle from plague, while the significance of Christ's crucifixion for our salvation is dwelt on in vivid and moving terms by the author of the work entitled variously *De Ligno Crucis*, *De Ligno Vitae* or *De Pascha* and by Venantius Fortunatus in his three famous hymns focusing on the cross, *Crux benedicta nitet*, *Pange, lingua, gloriosi proelium certaminis* (which contains the lines beginning *Crux fidelis* frequently set to music in the later Middle Ages) and *Vexilla regis prodeunt*.

The account of man's fall from grace (which necessitated Christ's death and resurrection) and its implications for the human condition are given in different forms not only in the poetic reworkings of the Genesis story by Cyprian the Poet, Claudius Marius Victorius and Avitus, but also in Prudentius' *Hamartigenia* (*The Origin of Sin*) and in Dracontius' *De Laudibus Dei*.[39] Satan takes centre stage in Book 2 of Avitus' work *De Spiritalis Historiae Gestis* (*The Spiritual History*), appearing also in the epics of Claudius Marius Victor and Cyprian the Poet, and in Prudentius' *Hamartigenia* (167–207). The theme of sin and its different forms is developed at length in Prudentius' *Psychomachia* (*Battle for the Soul*) and in the work of Orientius, the latter being not an epic but a poem of moral advice.

Paulinus of Nola, too, composed a few poems paraphrasing Scripture though these were on a smaller scale than the above-mentioned works of biblical epic: his Poem 6 is a panegyric on John the Baptist, expanded from the account in St Luke's Gospel, and he also wrote verse paraphrases of Psalms 1, 2 and 136.

Poems focusing on the lives of saints and martyrs include not only some of the hymns of Ambrose and the poems of Prudentius' *Peristephanon*, but also the poems by Paulinus of Nola composed annually for the feast-day of the third-century confessor Felix whose shrine was at Nola, some of the epigrams of Pope Damasus written to be inscribed at the shrines of certain saints at Rome and of Felix of Nola, and the long versified accounts of the life of St Martin of Tours, by Paulinus of Périgueux in the fifth century and by Venantius Fortunatus in the sixth, both basing their work on the prose *Life of Martin of Tours* by Sulpicius Severus. In his *Poem* 21 Paulinus of Nola gives an explanation of why such works were written:

> This is why the blessed martyrs whose perfect virtue has raised them to a heavenly crown gain the appropriate praise of honour due. We who succeed them in our confession of Christ's name all hymn them, for by shedding their blood for the holy faith they sowed the blessing of an eternal harvest, so that if we walk in the martyr's steps we can enjoy a reward equal to that of our progenitors.

Devotion to the saints and their relics, and celebration of their feast days developed during the course of the fourth century into an essential part of Christian life. These poems about saints and martyrs are therefore very much a product of their time (though their popularity would continue and even increase during the centuries to come). This is equally true of those poems dealing with heresy. The fourth century in particular is a time when the Christian Church was struggling to define its doctrine, to decide on what was orthodox and to suppress those beliefs it came to regard as erroneous and dangerous. At this stage doctrine could have been defined in a number of different ways and it is largely due to the strength and persistency of certain leading Christians, such as Athanasius, Basil, Gregory of Nazianzus and Gregory of Nyssa in the East and Ambrose, Augustine and Jerome in the West, that what came to be viewed as orthodoxy won through, overcoming Arians, Manichees, Pelagians and Donatists, all of which groups held views – either on the nature of the Trinity and of Christ, on sin and grace, or on the composition of the Church – which many found attractive at the time. Indeed, although these heresies were all condemned during the fourth and early fifth centuries, it was not always easy to stamp them out altogether: Pelagianism and Arianism in particular remained strong in parts of the Roman world during the following centuries, as we can see from some of the later poems written at the time to combat their beliefs.

In his poem *Apotheosis* Prudentius mentions the Manichees specifically (lines 956, 974) in connection with the belief that Christ did not take on a real body at the Incarnation, while in *Hamartigenia* he may have the Manichees in mind in his discussion of the origin of evil. The Manichees formed a sect that spread from Persia where their founder, Mani, had lived in the third century: despite condemnation and persecution this sect, with its complex cosmology and belief system based on dualism and only loosely connected with Christianity, flourished in the fourth century but gradually went into decline in the West over the next centuries. Its most famous adherent was Augustine who was a 'hearer' among the Manichees for about nine years, before becoming a passionate critic of their beliefs as his many writings against the sect show.[40]

A geographically more limited group was that of the Donatists, named by their opponents after Bishop Donatus; they caused a schism in the Church in North Africa which lasted through the fourth and into the early fifth century when Augustine's campaign against them resulted in their condemnation by an edict in 411. The schism had occurred after the terrible persecutions of 303–5 under the Emperor Diocletian: during these, many clergy in North Africa had lapsed and handed over the Scriptures to be burned, as demanded by the civil authorities. These priests had been regarded as traitors ('traditores') to the faith by those who had refused to submit. Such an intolerant attitude was not universal, however, and so there were soon two opposing camps formed from those who followed Donatus in believing that those who had lapsed needed to be rebaptized and that they themselves formed the true Church, and their opponents who held a less exclusive view of the Church. At the end of the fourth century Augustine was driven to formulate his views concerning the nature of the Church and its sacraments, including his belief that the Christian community in this world contains not only the pure, but both good and bad.[41] These are the views that he attempts to express in a popular form in his *Psalm against the Donatists*.

Another localized heresy which nevertheless was regarded as dangerous because it expressed a view of Christianity that many found seductive and that throughout the centuries of early Christianity and the Middle Ages threatened from time to time to erupt was Priscillianism, named after the fourth-century Bishop of Avila. His conversion to Christianity was accompanied by the choice of an ascetic lifestyle which in itself might have been no different from that adopted by other Christians of the period attracted to some form of the monastic life. However, Priscillian's use of certain texts used by the Manichees and the suspicion that he was guilty of sorcery finally led to his condemnation and execution, though there were many, such as Martin of Tours and Ambrose, who believed that the whole matter had been badly handled. At any rate, it would seem that even after his death in about 386, his views survived, for we have a work of Augustine against the Priscillianists dating from 415. It is perhaps not surprising then, that Prudentius, the Spanish poet, seems to be attacking Priscillianist doctrines, such as the belief that the soul is divine and that within the Trinity the Father and Son were not really distinct,[42] in his long poem *Apotheosis* (*The Divinity of Christ*) around the year 400.

Pelagianism was also condemned at very much the same period as Donatism but it offered an interpretation of Christian doctrine that was more subtly attractive and which was to linger on within Christianity for much longer than Donatism. The British priest Pelagius and his collaborator Celestius seem to have held that Adam's sin affected only himself, not the whole human race, and that man can take initial steps towards salvation by his own efforts, being free to choose the good by virtue of his God-given nature: these views led primarily to clashes on the question of man's nature, free will, and the need for grace, with Augustine again one of the leading opponents. With regard to poetry that touches on these issues, we have not only the explicitly anti-Pelagian work of Prosper of Aquitaine who was writing in the second quarter of the fifth century, but also, for example, Avitus's insistence in Book 1 of his *De Spiritalis Historiae Gestis*, written around the year 500, that Adam dooms his progeny, not only himself, when he sins.[43] This suggests that Pelagianism was still rife at this time, at least in southern Gaul where Avitus was bishop and this view is supported by the fact that the heresy had to be condemned again in 529 at the second Council of Orange. It is possible that a hint of sympathy for Pelagian views is detectable in the Prayer introducing the work of Claudius Marius Victorius who was writing at about the same time as Prosper of Aquitaine: the poet here defends the idea of human freedom.

Another major heresy which despite early condemnation survived well into the sixth century was Arianism: Arius' views had been rejected at the Council of Nicaea in 325, and yet Arianism had still to be repudiated by the third Council of Toledo in 589! Arian theology was based on the doctrine, aimed at protecting the monotheism of Christianity by safeguarding the unique divinity of God the Father, that the Son of God, the Word, is not eternal but was created out of nothing before time and that the Holy Spirit also lacks full divinity. Such a doctrine had significant implications for views on the nature of God, the nature of Christ, and the purpose and effectiveness of the Incarnation. The fact that it survived for so long was due not only to its superficial theological plausibility but also to the realities of ecclesiastical politics and to the adoption of Arian beliefs by the Goths who invaded the western empire in the fifth century. Arianism is more evident in early Christian Latin poetry than any other heresy, from the fourth century down to the sixth. Certainly some of the hymns of Hilary of Poitiers and of Ambrose were composed in response to the success of Arianism in the West in the second half of the fourth century and its survival in Gaul into the sixth century is apparent from the fact that the poet and bishop Avitus of Vienne was renowned for his work at this time in attempting to convert Arians to the Catholic faith.[44] We also have a psalm composed by Fulgentius of Ruspe in the early sixth century, explicitly directed against the Arians and modelled closely on Augustine's *Psalm against the Donatists*. Sedulius, in writing his *Carmen Paschale*, seems to have been largely motivated by the desire to put forward an anti-Arian view of Christ. He chooses to highlight those miracles in the Bible that prove that it was Christ's divinity, his equal status with the Father, that was at work in the marvellous events of the Old Testament and the New; even at the time of the Incarnation Christ is no mere man, but God as well as man. Briefer references are made to the Arian heresy by later writers such as Dracontius (2.95–110) and Arator (1.444, 918–919).

In the context of the attempt to formulate a coherent Christian doctrine from within the whirlpool of conflicting and often persuasive arguments that gave the Church a choppy passage through the fourth century and beyond, we might ask why so many poets were keen to treat the story of Genesis, in particular the account of Creation and the Fall. Although each poet handled the account differently, it is possible to generalize so far as to say that the writing of such poetry is likely to have been influenced by the fact that the early chapters of Genesis provided a site on which much doctrinal controversy was staged.[45] These poets may also have been motivated by a desire either to address the problem of the origin of evil, perhaps particularly after the fall of Rome to barbarian armies in 410 when it was clearly felt that the world was in a parlous state,[46] or to combat various forms of the Pelagian heresy which had a strong hold in Gaul during the fifth century. With regard to the problem of evil, already in the early third century Tertullian had written: 'The same subject matter is discussed over and over again by heretics and philosophers and the same arguments are involved: what is the origin of evil? Why is it permitted?'[47] But it would seem that a dualistic view, developed by such groups as the Gnostics and the Manichees, in which a sharp difference between the material world and the spiritual world was insisted on, as well as the existence of a demonic god, alongside a benevolent deity, who was responsible for the existence of evil, had a resurgence of popularity at the beginning of the fifth century. Prudentius, in his *Hamartigenia*, specifically combats the views of Marcion who had died 250 years earlier, but it is likely that he was aware that such views were still dangerously popular. Prudentius is keen to safeguard the doctrine of monotheism by stressing that it was no god, but a debased angel, who introduced evil into the world; admittedly there was a fine line between the orthodox doctrine of the devil and the Manichean teaching of a substantial principle of evil, and Augustine is characteristically careful to distinguish between them.[48] Other later writers who develop the Genesis account at greater length are concerned to show that the primal catastrophe of man's Fall was the cause of evil and misery, and that the material universe was inherently good, as J.M. Evans has shown in his book *Paradise Lost and the Genesis Tradition*.[49] It may be that the determination of such poets as Claudius Marius Victorius and Dracontius to emphasize God's benevolence amidst the awfulness of human existence may also be attributed to a concern to oppose a causative connection between God and evil. On the other hand, those writers who stress Adam and Eve's guilt – for example, Claudius Marius Victorius – may be trying to combat those like John Cassian who held views which could be termed semi-Pelagian, and who minimized the effects of Adam's disobedience in their belief that it was possible for people to do some good through the use of their free will, without the need for grace. It may be that some of these poets were also driven by a desire to create a Christian poetic version of the Creation story, obviously based on Genesis, to rival the accounts of Creation and the Golden Age in pagan literature, notably those of Lucretius in Book 5 of the *De Rerum Natura*, of Virgil in his fourth *Eclogue* and of Ovid in the first book of his *Metamorphoses*.

Although most of the poetry of this period is concerned with biblical material and Christian doctrine, there are poems that are more personal but nevertheless strongly Christian. There is the poetry that attempts to offer consolation based on Christian beliefs. This is exemplified by three lengthy poems: Paulinus of Nola's poem addressed to the parents of a boy who died at the age of 8, by Venantius Fortunatus' verses addressed to Chilperic, king of the Franks (himself a writer of poems which according to Gregory of Tours[50] were poor imitations of Sedulius) on the death of his two young sons, and by Avitus' poem to his sister, the prime motive of which is to encourage her in her dedication to a life of chastity and console her for the lack of husband, children and the trappings of secular life.

Paulinus of Nola is also the author of the only extant epithalamium or wedding song from the period that is explicitly Christian: his *Poem* 25 is written for the marriage of a certain Julian, later Bishop of Eclanum, who was to become Augustine's powerful opponent in the Pelagian controversy. In this wedding song Paulinus rejects all the traditional mythological paraphernalia: out go Venus, Cupid and the nymphs, to be replaced by Christ, out goes the promotion of the sexual relationship to be replaced by an emphasis on chastity and friendship within marriage in an extraordinary reversal of the traditional themes associated with this genre. Other Christians, such as Dracontius (poems 6 and 7), Ennodius (Book 1, poem 4) and Venantius Fortunatus (Book 6, poem 1), were to write epithalamia but they all did so with the traditional pagan ornamentation.

Another long poem is that by Paulinus of Pella, a poem of autobiography written to record the poet's gratitude to God for his past life despite all the misfortunes he has suffered.

Then there are the poems of Christian friendship, as for example those written by Paulinus of Nola to his friend and mentor Ausonius, in which he tries tactfully to make it clear that now that he is committed to Christianity he no longer holds the same values as Ausonius, or the occasional verses addressed to friends, often bishops, clergymen and nuns, by Venantius Fortunatus on various subjects related to Christian life, whether flower arrangements in church or the celebration of Easter.

Given the varieties of literary genre and content within this committedly Christian corpus of poetry, is it possible to summarize its dominant stylistic traits? As already mentioned, these poets stand firmly in the classical tradition of imitation and adaptation of earlier works of literature. However, this fact has been largely neglected by recent scholars writing about imitation of the classical poets: typical of this restricted vision is the recent work of Philip Hardie, *The Epic Successors of Virgil*[51] which deals with no poet between the end of the first century and the Renaissance. Even when such imitation is noticed, it is regarded as a sign of the Christian poets' decadence and lack of originality. And yet the early Christian Latin poets' use of the metres of classical poetry and their reworking of the poems of Lucretius, Virgil, Ovid, Statius and Lucan in particular, put them in the same tradition as many of the earlier Latin poets who had made similar use of Homer, the Greek lyric poets or the Hellenistic Greek poets. It is hardly just to criticize the Christian poets for their ubiquitous use of Virgil (especially in those cases where the Christian poets created works of depth and originality), when Virgil had had a similar approach to both the Homeric epics, while later Latin poets were very conscious of their debt to Virgil. However, even if one regards imitation as a sign of weakness, one should not tar all the poets with the same brush. At one extreme we have Proba's *Cento*, a literary curiosity which even her contemporaries considered more notable for its ingenuity than for any talent.[52] Then we may pass through the biblical epics of Juvencus and Sedulius which use much Virgilian language, the epic of Arator, with, for example, its account of St Paul's shipwreck, and that of Prudentius with his *Psychomachia* depicting the battle of the Vices and Virtues in Virgilian terms, to a looser use of Virgil, alongside Statius and Lucan, by Dracontius and Avitus.

Imitation of Virgil may be one of the most striking characteristics of much of early Christian Latin poetry, but in many cases a deeper exploration of this will reveal many interesting differences and possible intentional ironies[53] as well as similarities and absurdities. Furthermore, if we do examine these poems closely and do not simply write them off as incompetent imitations, we find that in many of them the traditional poetic tropes and figures of speech, such as metaphors and imagery, allegory and personification, are employed to give the text a figurative meaning underlying the literal account.

This reflects not only the pagan use of allegory (regarded by Augustine, for example, as inferior to Christian allegory on the grounds that the texts allegorized contained less truth than the Bible) but the development of Christian biblical exegesis in which allegory came to be applied to explain difficult passages of Scripture: this development took place in the West particularly under the influence of Jerome, who translated some of Origen's exegetical works, and of Hilary of Poitiers and Ambrose who used their knowledge of Greek methods of interpretation in their own exegesis.[54] Typology was used to bring out the significant connections between events and characters in the Old Testament and the New: since according to orthodox interpretation Christianity was based on the belief that by his Incarnation Christ fulfilled the promises and reversed the negative aspects of the Old Testament dispensation, Christian writers were able to exploit the correspondences they saw between the Old Testament and the New, especially in connection with Adam's fall from grace and Christ's redemption. Had not Christ said, 'Do not think that I have come to abolish the law or the prophets. I have come not to abolish but to fulfil,' (Matthew 5:17)? An example of such a typological interpretation is Avitus' linking of the creation of Eve from Adam's rib with the creation of the Church from the wound in Christ's side: such an allegorical interpretation of Christ's wounding on the cross could be found in Augustine's *Tractates on the Gospel of John*, where he writes that, 'from the wound flowed the sacraments of the Church' (i.e. the blood of the Eucharist and the waters of baptism) . . . 'This was announced beforehand when . . . the first woman was formed from the side of the man when asleep, and was called Life, the mother of all living.'[55] Metaphor had of course been used in the Bible, too, as when Christ says to the Samaritan woman:

> Whoever drinks this water will be thirsty again; but no one who drinks the water that I shall give him will ever be thirsty again; the water that I shall give him will become in him a spring of water, welling up for eternal life
>
> (John 4:13–14)

and Christ's use of parables also helped to steer Christian writers towards a figurative interpretation of the text. In this way pagan poetics harmonized satisfactorily with Christian exegesis, allowing for great hermeneutic richness. In the *Carmen Paschale*, for example, Sedulius not only puts Christ's Incarnation, death and resurrection at the climax of the poem, but also selects those scriptural passages he considers typologically significant as indicating the fulfilment of God's plan for mankind. The poet also hints at correspondences by the way he describes a character or event, as when he gives a picture of Judas, at the betrayal of Christ, in terms of Satan's seduction of Adam and Eve.[56] In Arator's poem, the literal account from the Acts of the Apostles alternates with a spiritual interpretation that seeks to reveal the significance of the passage in theological, doctrinal or moral terms.[57] This method of interpretation is fundamental to the literature of the period in the West and will continue to be so, and to be further developed, through the course of the Middle Ages.[58]

Michael Roberts[59] has shown that another characteristic of much Christian poetry of this period is the paraphrasing of the text the poet is handling, a skill he would have learnt in his rhetoric lessons, enabling him to rephrase the text in a new form, abbreviating or expanding it at will. Again, as in the interpretation of the text, the notable fact is that the poets are so often working with a given text, whether the Bible or the works of the pagan poets, or a given set of doctrines, rather than creating *ex nihilo*. The manner in which each poet reworks the text, for example, in his adaptation of the order of events, as in much of the poetry on Genesis, can help the reader to understand the poet's purpose.

Along with the style of the poems, we must give a brief account of the verse forms used by these poets, although this is a controversial area in which much work remains to be done on the individual authors. To summarize, one might say that most of this poetry continued to be written in the quantitative metres of Classical Antiquity, with the dactylic hexameter being by far the most common. This is not surprising, considering the number of poems which might be considered as forms of epic, for which the hexameter was the traditional metre in Greek and Latin literature. Even in the sixth century Arator and Venantius Fortunatus were still able to write what are regarded as 'proper' hexameters. Other metres used by these poets were elegiac couplets as in the case of Lactantius' *Phoenix* and Orientius' *Commonitorium* (*A work of admonition*), trochaic septenarii (also known as the trochaic tetrameter catalectic, a metre originally associated with soldiers' marching songs) used by Hilary (*Adae carnis gloriosae et caduci corporis*), Prudentius in his *Peristephanon* 1 which opens with the line *Scripta sunt caelo duorum martyrum vocabula*, and Venantius Fortunatus (*Pange, lingua, gloriosi proelium certaminis*) in their hymns; asclepiads, modelled perhaps on Horace, Odes 1.1 or 1.6, as exemplified by the preface to the first book of Prudentius' *Contra Symmachum* or by the *Eclogue* of Endelechius, and sapphics as we find in Prudentius' *Cathemerinon* 8 and in Venantius Fortunatus' poem 9.7. One metre which was to become very popular was the iambic dimeter, used by Ambrose for all his hymns and subsequently chosen by many writers of hymns, from Prudentius in some of his *Cathemerinon* poems (hymns 1, 11 and 12), written shortly after Ambrose's hymns, on through the following centuries. Ambrose still followed the strict quantitative rules for this metre – whereby word accent does not on the whole coincide with the metrical beat, and elision between words does occur – but it soon came to be adapted to a rhythmic form of unstressed and stressed syllables which was to make this four-line stanza form one of the most popular poetic forms during the Middle Ages.

With regard to the rhythmic metres that were to dominate in the Latin Middle Ages, we see the first beginnings in the poetry of this period: Commodian seems to have written his two poems, the *Instructiones* and the *Carmen Apologeticum* (or *Carmen de duobus populis*) in rhythmic hexameters which Gennadius writing in the fifth century refers to as 'a kind of verse', while Augustine consciously chose to use a non-quantitative form, based on a sixteen-syllable line, for his *Psalm against the Donatists* because he believed this would make his verse more accessible to his congregation. Various suggestions have been put forward as to why quantitative verse was gradually to a large extent superseded by rhythmic verse: it may be that with the influx of foreigners into the Roman Empire of late antiquity the pronunciation of Latin altered, so that even if the poets of this period continued to write quantitative verse it was no longer based on the pronunciation of their day; or the accentual system of rhythmic verse may have been latent in Latin throughout its history but was only brought to the surface by Christianity with its roots in popular culture; or thirdly, rhythmical verse may have been entirely new to Latin, owing its popularity to the influence of Syriac hymns whose form depended on the numbering of syllables, alphabetical arrangements and grouping into strophes.

Two characteristics of later Latin verse that first make tentative and fitful appearances during this period are the use of rhyme which by the twelfth century was to become highly developed but at this stage was hardly obvious, and the use of acrostics in verse (as, for example, by Commodian and by Venantius Fortunatus) which was to become particularly popular in the early medieval period and the Carolingian age.

Given the modern lack of interest in these poets, it may be surprising to find that many of them attained great popularity during the Middle Ages – among those who were sufficiently well educated to read them. As education in Latin became increasingly restricted to the monasteries, it was primarily monks who studied these works; a number of these poems soon became part of the curriculum, alongside the works of certain classical pagan poets. It is possible to estimate the popularity of a work from the number of times it is mentioned or alluded to by other writers, or from references to the work as existing in medieval library catalogues. Isidore of Seville, at the beginning of the seventh century, refers to Juvencus, Prudentius, Sedulius, Avitus and Arator as being available in his library, and in fact it was the poets of biblical epic who were particularly widely read, and who influenced such works in the vernacular as the Old English *Genesis B* and the Gospels of Otfrid von Weissenburg in Old German, both dating from the ninth century. It was the works of these poets which also provided examples for the writers of grammatical textbooks, as is particularly evident from the grammars by Irish and English writers of the early Middle Ages. Alcuin at the end of the eighth century gives a more comprehensive list of Christian authors in his poem on the church at York, mentioning Avitus, Prudentius, Sedulius, Juvencus, Prosper of Aquitaine, Paulinus of Nola, Arator, Lactantius and Venantius Fortunatus. Among the works of Prudentius and Prosper it was the *Psychomachia* of the former and the epigrams of the latter that seem to have been best known: the *Psychomachia* with its use of allegorical personifications was particularly influential on literature of the later Middle Ages. Dracontius' *De Laudibus Dei* seems to have been less widely read except in the abbreviated version made by Eugenius of Toledo in about 650. Ambrose's hymns remained well known throughout the Middle Ages, and inspired the writing of innumerable hymns in the same form.

It is to be hoped that this attempt to put the poetic works of this period – which has been regarded variously as the end of antiquity and the beginning of the Middle Ages – into the context of an 'objective' literary history, giving some idea of the theological issues involved, will provide readers of the poems and extracts translated here (many of them for the first time) with a basic introduction that might inspire them to explore further the delights and complexities of this unjustly neglected corpus.

# Part 2

# TRANSLATIONS

# LACTANTIUS

## Introduction

The 170-line poem telling the story of the mythical phoenix, translated here in full, has been convincingly attributed to Lactantius,[1] the Christian writer born in North Africa around the middle of the third century, who was converted to Christianity, survived the persecutions under the Emperor Diocletian at the beginning of the fourth century, and ended up as tutor to the Emperor Constantine's son at Trier during the very first years when Christianity was becoming an officially accepted religion. He is famed not so much for this poem as for his prose works of Christian apologetics written in an urbane style that appealed to the humanists of the Renaissance who referred to him as 'the Christian Cicero'. His prose writings include the *Divinae Institutiones* (*The Divine Institutes*) and works entitled *De Ira Dei* (*The Anger of God*), *De Opificio Dei* (*The Workmanship of God*), and *De Mortibus Persecutorum* (*The Deaths of the Persecutors*) in which Lactantius, more of a rhetorician than a theologian, is concerned to show the inaccuracy of pagan philosophical views regarding the nature of God and of human beings, and to discuss the question of where true wisdom and virtue are to be found.

The poem on the phoenix is based on the oriental myth of the phoenix, the bird which is supposed to live for many hundreds of years and then bring about its own death by means of which it is born again. The myth was told throughout antiquity, appearing in different forms in the works of such writers as Herodotus, Ovid and Pliny.[2] Among Christians it is clear that the myth was seized upon either as providing a symbol of resurrection in the natural world, as an analogy to Christ's resurrection, or was interpreted typologically as applying to Christ:[3] Christ, like the phoenix, could be regarded as coming from a country in the East, namely paradise, to a country where death holds sway, and after suffering death and experiencing resurrection he goes back whence he came, namely, to God the Father. Although the poem here is not specifically Christian and no analogy is drawn between the phoenix and Christ, there are certain indications that the author had a Christian interpretation of the myth in mind: for example, four times the poet uses the symbolically significant number twelve; the description of the phoenix's home in the east is reminiscent of the description of paradise in the early chapters of Genesis; and the reference to the place where death holds sway (line 64) has scriptural overtones.

## Text

Example of Latin verse form; elegiac couplets

*The Phoenix*, lines 1–4

Est locus in primo felix oriente remotus
    Qua patet aeterni maxima porta poli,
Nec tamen aestivos hiemisve propinquus ad ortus,
    Sed qua Sol verno fundit ab axe diem.

The Latin text from which the translation is taken is that of M. C. Fitzpatrick (1933). The text of the poem is also given in CSEL 27 (1893). It has been translated not only by Fitzpatrick but also in volume 7 of the *Ante-Nicene Fathers* (T. and T. Clark, Edinburgh, repr. 1994) and by M. F. McDonald in FC 54 (Washington, DC, 1965).

## The Phoenix

There lies a place far off, on the eastern edge of the world,
A blessed place, where the great portal of the eternal skies
    stands open:
This place does not lie close to the sun's rising in summer or
    winter
But close to the point where it pours light from its chariot in
    spring.
There a plateau extends over a wide area,
And no hill rises nor hollow valley opens out.
This place lies twelve metres above our world's mountains,
The summits of which are considered very high.

Here grows the forest of the sun, a sacred grove planted
10  Thick with trees, glorying in its evergreen foliage.
    When the fires of Phaethon[4] caused a conflagration in the sky
    That place remained undamaged by the flames,
    And when the Flood drowned the world beneath its waves,
    That place stood out above the waters of Deucalion.[5]
    To this place come no pale diseases, nor sickly old age,
    Neither cruel death nor pitiless fear haunt that place.
    Here come no wicked crimes nor greed, mad for wealth,
    Nor frenzy, burning with a desire to kill.
    Bitter grief is absent and so is ragged need;
20  N o sleepless cares exist there nor violent hunger.
    No storm blows there nor the wind's wild force,
    No frost covers the earth with its icy dew,
    No cloud stretches its woolly wisps over these plains,
    And no downpours of rain fall on it from on high.
    But in its midst is found a fountain, clear and gentle,
    Abounding in sweet waters and called the living spring.
    It wells up once each month, twelve times a year
    It floods the whole grove with its waters.
    Here grows a species of tree, rising up with a long trunk
30  And bearing juicy fruit that never falls to the ground.
    A unique bird, the phoenix, inhabits this forest, these groves,
    But though unique she lives reborn through her own death,
    A remarkable attendant for Phoebus whom she obediently
          serves.
    On this bird Mother Nature has bestowed this privilege:
    As soon as saffron Dawn rises and begins to blush,
    As soon as she puts the stars to flight with her rosy light,
    Twelve times the bird plunges into the sacred pool,
    Twelve times she sips the water from the living spring.
    Next she flies up and settles on a tall tree's topmost branch,
40  – the only one providing a view of the whole grove –
    Then turns towards the new dawn as Phoebus rises
    And awaits his rays as his light climbs above the horizon.
    And when the sun has knocked on the door of the shining
          portal
    And the first light's faint gleam has flickered through,
    The bird begins to pour out the melody of her sacred song
    To summon the new day with a wondrous sound,
    Unmatched by the song of the nightingale
    Or the Cirrhaean measure of the Muses' flute;

Not even the dying swan could be thought to rival it
50  Nor could the melodious strings of Mercury's lyre.
When Phoebus has allowed his horses to rush out into the open
    skies,
Illuminating the whole world as he journeys up and on,
Then thrice the bird flaps her wings to express approval
And after thrice paying homage to the sun's fiery head, she is
    silent.
Then this same bird with her indescribably beautiful song
Marks out the fleeting hours of day and night,
She who is guardian of the forest, revered priestess of the grove,
Sole sharer, Phoebus, of your secrets.
When she has completed her thousand years of life,
60  It is as if she finds her long life oppressive.
She leaves the familiar groves, the nest she loves
To renew the life slipping away in her declining years.
Eager to be reborn she leaves the sacred place
And wings her way towards this world where death holds sway.
The long-lived bird flies swiftly in the direction of Syria
To which she herself long ago gave the name Phoenicia:
Over pathless deserts she makes for secluded groves,
Looking among the hills for a far-off wood, concealed.
Next she chooses a tall palm tree, reaching high into the air,
70  A tree deriving its Greek name, phoenix, from this bird.
Into this tree can creep no harmful creature,
Whether slippery snake or any bird of prey.
Then Aeolus imprisons the winds in their vaulted caverns
In case they should disturb the calm air with their gusts
Or a cloud condensed by the south wind in the clear skies
Should block the sun's rays and obstruct the bird.
Then she builds herself a nest or rather, a tomb,
For she dies so as to live since she can recreate herself.
Here she collects juices and perfumes from the fruitful wood,
80  Like those the Assyrians gather or rich Arabians,
Like those the pygmy people or Indians pick
Or those the land of Sheba produces in its soft bosom.
Here she piles up cinnamon, amomum with its wide-spread
    scent
And balsam combined with leaves of nard,
Sweet cassia bark, too, and fragrant acanthus twigs,
As well as tears of incense with its rich drops.
To these the bird adds tender shoots of nard, filled with sap,

Combining your efficacy, panacea, with myrrh.
Now she settles her body, ready to change, on the nest she has
    built,
90   Resting her relaxed limbs on the life-giving bed.
With her beak she sprinkles juices around and over her body,
Planning to die at the funeral she herself has arranged.
Then amidst all the various scents she gives up her life,
Not fearing to relinquish such a valuable deposit.
Meanwhile her body, destroyed by a life-giving death,
Grows hot and of itself the heat gives out a flame,
Catching fire from the heavenly sunlight far away:
It blazes forth and as it burns up it disintegrates.
Creating life in death, nature fuses these ashes
100 Into a sort of lump, producing something like a seed.
From this, they say, emerges first a living creature without
    limbs,
And it is said the colour of this worm is milky white.
It grows and after a fixed period it sleeps,
Forming itself into the shape of a smooth round egg,
Like grubs in the country that cling to stones by a thread,
Waiting to be transformed into butterflies;
From this grub it produces once more its original form
And as it bursts open the chrysalis, the phoenix emerges.
In this world there is no food provided for her
110 Nor is anyone at hand to feed the unfledged bird.
She sips the ambrosial dews of heavenly nectar,
A delicate drink that falls from the starry sky:
This the bird collects, on this she feeds amid the scents
Until she is ready to appear in fully-grown form.
But when she begins to grow strong, in the first years of her
    youth,
She flies away, now planning to return to her home.
But first, whatever remains of her own body,
Bones or ashes and her own chrysalis,
She covers in balsam ointment, myrrh and incense of Sheba
120 And rounds it into shape with her loving beak.
Carrying it in her claws she hastens to where the sun rises
And lays it in the holy shrine as she perches on the altar.
She presents herself to be wondered at and worshipped,
So beautiful is the bird, so distinguished, inspiring admiration.
Firstly the colour of pomegranates at the height of summer,
Covering their seeds with a skin of saffron hue,

The colour on petals of poppies in country fields
When Flora spreads her skirt over the reddening land:
These are the bright colours gleaming on her neck and breast,
130 These colours shine from her head, neck and back.
She spreads her tail, speckled with yellow gold
And glowing with purple mixed in with the markings.
Her wing feathers are marked by Iris the rainbow
Whose colours often paint the clouds from above.
Her beak of pure ivory opens, set with precious stones:
It is of radiant whiteness, shot with emerald green.
Her eyes are huge: you would think them twin sapphires
From the centre of which flash forth bright flames.
To her remarkable head a circle of rays has been fitted,
140 A lofty circlet, reflecting the fire of Phoebus' crown.
Scales cover her legs, speckled with yellow gold,
While a lovely rosy colour tinges her claws.
In appearance she resembles something between
A peacock and a richly coloured pheasant.
That winged creature which is born in Arabian lands[6] –
Is it a bird or not? – scarcely equals the phoenix in size.
Yet she is not sluggish like those large-bodied birds,
Advancing slowly because of their great weight;
She is light and swift and full of regal beauty,
150 This is how she always appears to people.
The Egyptians flock here to witness this great marvel
And the crowd greets this rare bird with cheers.
At once they carve her shape in sacred marble
And mark the day and the event with a new inscription.
Every kind of bird gathers together there,
Some forget their prey, the others forget their fear.
Surrounded by winged creatures, the phoenix flies through the
   sky
Escorted by the crowd, which is happy to perform this act of
   devotion.
But on reaching the pure air of heaven, the flock of birds
160 Turns back and the phoenix disappears to her own domain.
O blessed bird, what a fortunate fate is yours,
Whom God has enabled to be born from yourself!
Whether the bird is female or male or neither,
Blessed it is, for it practises no sexual union.
Death is for her the sexual act, in death lies her sole pleasure.
So that she may be reborn, she knows she first must die.

She is her own offspring, her own father and heir,
She is her own nurse and always her own foster child.
She remains herself but not the same, the same but not herself,
170 Gaining through the gift of death life everlasting.

# JUVENCUS

## Introduction

Juvencus' poem in four books on the life of Christ, from which two excerpts are translated here, was written around the year 330. According to Jerome[1] Juvencus was a Spaniard of noble family who lived under the Emperor Constantine. He based his poem on the four Gospels, apparently giving a more or less literal, and very restrained, paraphrase of them in hexameter verse.[2] He follows the order of the Old Latin or *Itala* text of the Bible faithfully, drawing most of his material from St Matthew's Gospel[3] not only to describe Christ's miracles but also to give summaries of his parables and culminating with Christ's passion and resurrection in Book 4.

In the preface to the poem Juvencus outlines his purpose in writing: nothing in this world is everlasting but great deeds and writings can live on through the work of poets as in the case of Homer and Virgil. If poems such as these, with fictitious subjects, can endure through the ages, how much more so must it be the case with this poem of Juvencus which deals with facts that are definitely true. The poet hopes also that his poem will win not only fame for himself, but even salvation, saving him from the fires of hell at the Last Judgement.[4] It is often suggested that Juvencus' motive for writing was his desire to replace the pagan epics with a Christian one which still had the beauty and attractiveness of the older works, but this motive is not one that Juvencus emphasizes. It is true that instead of alluding to the Muses and their spring as the source of his poetic inspiration, Juvencus calls on the Holy Spirit and refers to the waters of the River Jordan. Yet his language and style remain resolutely in the pagan literary mould, influenced largely by Virgil, but also by Lucretius and Statius; following in their footsteps he even creates some epic neologisms, such as *auricolor* (golden-coloured), *flammivomus* (spewing flames) and *altithronus* (enthroned on high). Though poetic, his style is clear and straightforward; the alliteration often mentioned by critics is by no means a dominant feature.

Juvencus was one of the most widely read poets of the Middle Ages and yet little interest has been shown in modern times in the content of Juvencus' poem. Although he treats the biblical material in a more literal way than many later writers, such as Sedulius or Avitus, and keeps closely to the text he is paraphrasing, it is nevertheless possible to see the poet giving a certain slant to his account: Juvencus is clearly interested in the theme of prophecy and points out anything related to this theme at every possible opportunity. Christ is seen as fulfilling the prophecies of the Old Testament, which Juvencus often alludes to or summarizes (e.g. at 3.144). Christ is himself a prophet, whose words must be taken seriously and who by his miracles provides signs that what he says will come true; Juvencus also emphasizes John the Baptist's role as a prophet foretelling the coming of Christ. Juvencus is concerned not merely to produce an epic with Christian content to replace the popular pagan epics, but to show that Christ brings salvation and everlasting life to those who believe in him. Christ's deeds and words (and Juvencus includes much direct speech which enlivens the epic) bring life – the poet refers to Christ as 'the sole hope of life' (3.521). In Book 4 much is made of Christ's eschatological speech in Chapter 24 of St Matthew's Gospel, whereby the reader's attention is forcibly directed to the next world and the question of his own spiritual future.

The passages chosen for translation give Juvencus' versions of the coming of the Magi to see the infant Jesus, and of the Last Supper.

## Texts

Latin text: CSEL 24 (1891); PL 19.

Example of Latin verse form; hexameters

Preface, lines 1–5

Immortale nihil mundi compage tenetur,
Non orbis, non regna hominum, non aurea Roma,
Non mare, non tellus, non ignea sidera caeli.
Nam statuit genitor rerum irrevocabile tempus,
Quo cunctum torrens rapiat flamma ultima mundum.

## Poem on the Gospels 1.224–254

*Based on Matthew 2:1–12*

There is a people far away that knows the secrets of the rising
    sun,
Skilled at noting the risings and settings of the stars:
Magi was the name given to their leading men.
At that time chosen ones from this country made the long
    journey
To reach Jerusalem: they approached the king, asking for
    information
As to the region of Judea where there lived a child
230  Born to rule. They said they had been inspired to make the
    journey
By the appearance of a bright star, so that with suppliant
    hands
They might worship the divine power revealed to the world.
Herod was terrified and summoned the chief priests in
    Jerusalem
And those who studied the ancient sayings of the prophets.
He ordered them to search through everything in the Torah
To find out which city was to be the birthplace of Christ
Whose coming had been foretold in all the prophecies.
It then became clear that it was in the town of Bethlehem
That the birth was expected of the one who was to lead
240  The holy people of Israel, scrupulous in their virtue.[5]
Then Herod ordered the Persians to continue on their way
And show him the child they find so that he might worship
    him.
And look! They saw the star moving before them right above
    their path,
Cutting a furrow through the air with its flames until it halted
At the zenith, pointing out the child's dwelling upon which it
    shone.
The Magi rejoiced with great joy and welcomed the star
And when they saw the child at his mother's breast
They fell to the ground, prostrating themselves,
And prayed together in supplication. Then they offered
250  Three gifts – frankincense, gold and myrrh – as presents for
    him
As God, as king, as man.[6] But throughout the next night

They were disturbed by nightmares warning them to avoid the
    cruel king.
And in fact the Magi took a different route and fled
From Herod's palace, returning in secret to their native land.


## 4.428– 477

*Based on Matthew 26:17–35*

And now the first day of the Passover had dawned:
The disciples inquired where Christ would like to eat
430 The Passover meal; but he told them to find a man he does not
    name
Who would carry out the Lord's final orders.
That evening, as soon as the twelve disciples sat down together,
Their master spoke to them in these words of things to come:
'Now the time is almost upon us when one of you
is wickedly planning to hand Christ over to death.'
At once they all asked him who would dare do such a thing?
Who was mad enough to conceive such a poisonous idea?
Then Christ replied, 'He is now eating this meal with me.
But the Son of Man will undergo those sufferings for a short
    while,
440 As laid down long ago, while he who betrays the one who is
    just
Will be in torment for ever. How much happier would he have
    been
If he had never experienced the light of life on earth!'
Then Judas, whose guilty conscience was causing him deep
    anguish,
Said, 'Surely it is not Judas whom you suspect?'
The Lord replied, 'It is you whom I see saying this.'
When he had spoken thus he broke the bread with his hands,
And divided it up, solemnly blessed it and handed it out,
Telling his disciples that they were thereby eating his own body.
Then the Lord took the cup and filled it with wine,
450 Consecrated it with words of thanksgiving and handed round
    the drink,
Telling them that he was sharing out his own blood.
He said, 'This blood has paid for the sins of the people.
Drink this – it is mine. For you must believe the truth of my
    words;

After this I will never again taste the juice of the vine
Until it is granted me through the gift of a better life
To rise again and drink new wines in my Father's kingdom.'
Next, when they had sung a hymn in sacred harmony,
Together they all climbed up the Mount of Olives.
Then Christ poured out these words from his heart,
460 'All of you, during this present night, will be driven by fear
To scatter far and wide, wretchedly deserting your leader.
For thus it is written: as a result of the shepherd's misfortune,
All the sheep will scatter across the fields in different
    directions.[7]
But afterwards when life has granted me new honours in
    heaven,
I shall go before you and I will teach your flocks
As I move about through Galilee's pleasant countryside.'
Peter answered, 'If we must believe you, everyone else
May have doubts and refuse to obey your commands,
But no danger will ever make me change my allegiance.'
470 Then Christ replied, 'This night that draws the shining stars
Over the earth, concealing the light, and now broods upon the
    waves,
Will hear how you, in fear, three times will tell a lie.
For all your courage, Peter, you will yet deny Christ
Before the rooftops echo with the crowing of the cock.'
But Peter answered, 'I would prefer to suffer a painful death
Rather than that I should forget my master and deny him in
    my words.'
And they all persisted in promising equal strength of mind.

# PROBA

## Introduction

The only work extant by the aristocratic Roman lady Faltonia Betitia Proba is her *Cento*, or 'patchwork' poem, of 694 hexameters, written in about 360. Furthermore, very little is known about the identity of this woman: it is possible that she is identical with the Proba who is the addressee of one letter from Augustine and one from John Chrysostom.[1] Her poem is composed entirely of a hotch-potch of lines and half-lines, occasionally slightly altered, from the works of Virgil. In using only Virgilian lines, Proba's work takes the tendency of Christian poets to find their main inspiration in Virgil to its logical, and sometimes absurd, extreme. Lines 1–332 give an account based on the Old Testament stories of the Creation and Fall down to the Flood, while lines 333–694 are based on the New Testament and tell of Christ's ministry, death and resurrection by which mankind is redeemed from the effects of the Fall.

Proba's poem is by far the most famous poem of its kind but not the only one. There exist also a cento derived from Virgil's pastoral poems which takes the form of a dialogue between a pagan and a Christian, and two on the Incarnation and the Church respectively.[2] Proba's cento was particularly popular during the Renaissance, no doubt because of the great respect it shows for Virgil.

The passage excerpted and translated below gives an account of the Last Supper which follows the events of Matthew 26:20ff. but describes them in terms largely of Aeneas' feasting with Dido on his arrival at Carthage. References to the lines of Virgil are given in the notes.

## Text

Latin text: CSEL 16 (1888) 569–609; PL 19.805-818.

Example of Latin verse form; hexameters

Lines 1–8

Iam dudum temerasse duces pia foedera pacis,
Regnandi miseros tenuit quos dira cupido,
Diversasque neces, regum crudelia bella
Cognatasque acies, pollutos caede parentum
Insignis clipeos nulloque ex hoste tropaea,
Sanguine conspersos tulerat quos fama triumphos,
Innumeris totiens viduatas civibus urbes,
Confiteor, scripsi, satis est meminisse malorum.

## Cento 580–599

*Loosely based on Matthew 26:20–24*

580 Meanwhile evening draws on, moving down Olympus' slopes.[3]
Then they restore their strength with food: stretched out on the grass[4]
They load the tables with dishes and set out the cups.[5]
When first there was a lull in the feasting and the tables were cleared,[6]
He himself among the foremost[7] performed the rites in his father's honour,[8]
Lifting his eyes to heaven.[9] Then silence fell on all their tongues.[10]
He shares out the bread with his hands,[11] as well as fresh spring water[12]
And fills the cup with wine,[13] telling them of the sacred rites.[14]
He includes some prayers, too,[15] and speaks to them thus:[16]
'Listen, princes,' he said, 'and learn of your hopes.[17]
590 None of those present here will depart without a gift from me:[18]
Trust in my father's promises;[19] your rewards remain assured to you,[20]
My lads, for no one will alter the order of your prizes.[21]
As soon as tomorrow's dawn returns to earth,[22]

One only will there be,[23] who seeks to destroy me and my
      people,[24]
When he pushes his way into our midst to kiss me.[25]
For now, unless I am mistaken, the day is at hand.[26] Away with
      your cares.[27]
With me will rest this task,[28] and my judgement does not err:[29]
One life will be sacrificed for many.'[30] So saying[31]
He fell silent[32] and allowed sleep at last to steal over his
      limbs.[33]

# DAMASUS

## Introduction

Damasus, who was pope at Rome from 366 to 384, was born in about 305 into a Christian family. His papacy was a troubled one but he managed to achieve an enormous amount, despite the difficulties of dealing with an anti-pope (Ursinus) and many different sects at Rome. Damasus worked hard to promote the primacy of Rome over all other sees, believing the Bishop of Rome to be the direct successor of St Peter. He was not, however, as energetic in promoting good relations with the Church in the eastern empire, failing, for example, to attend the Council of Constantinople in 381. And yet he did help to suppress Arianism, advanced the cult of the martyrs, and launched many church construction projects in Rome which served to turn the city from the centre of a pagan empire to the centre of the Christian Church. He also commissioned Jerome to work on the revision of the Latin text of the Bible, a work which would eventually result in the Vulgate text superseding the Old Latin, or *Itala*, text. Furthermore, he was cultivated and on good terms with the aristocracy: in fact his magnificent lifestyle helped to attract upper-class pagans to Christianity at a time when this was very necessary for the survival of the Church. All in all, this man, who was pope at such an exciting period of the Church's development, was instrumental in laying a firm foundation for the Church in many crucial areas.

As for his writings, it has been suggested that Damasus contributed to the early parts of the document known as the *Decretum Gelasianum* dealing with the sources of the Church's authority, though the work as a whole is a product of the sixth century. A number of Damasus' letters are extant, including a few addressed to Jerome. Damasus also composed doctrinal statements, and Jerome states that he wrote on the subject of virginity in prose and verse.[1] He was also the author of a number of epigrams, 59 of which are now regarded as genuine, mostly written to be engraved on marble on the tombs of martyrs at Rome. Of these I have translated the epitaph Damasus wrote for himself, and his epitaph on St Agnes.[2]

## Texts

Latin text: PL 13; *Epigrammata Damasiana* (ed. A. Ferrua, Rome, 1942).

Example of Latin verse form; hexameters

*Epigram 12*

> Qui gradiens pelagi fluctus compressit amaros,
> Vivere qui prestat morientia semina terrae,
> Solvere qui potuit letalia vincula mortis
> Post tenebras, fratrem post tertia lumina solis
> Ad superos iterum Martae donare sorori,
> Post cineres Damasum faciet quia surgere credo.

## Epigram 12

*His own epitaph*

> He who walked upon the salt sea waves and stilled them,
> He who can make dying seeds come to life in the earth,
> He who could burst asunder the deadly chains of death
> And after three nights of darkness, three days of light
> Give back to Martha, the sister, her brother restored to life,
> He, I believe, is able to make Damasus rise again after death.

## Epigram 37

*Inscription on St Agnes*

> According to tradition, some time ago her devout parents
>     reported
> That when the trumpet summoned her with its mournful
>     melody,
> Their daughter Agnes suddenly left her nurse's bosom;
> Voluntarily she scorned the cruel tyrant's threats and rage

When he decided to burn her noble body in the flames:
Despite her weakness he failed to inspire in her a powerful fear.
She let her hair flow down over her naked body
So that no mortal man should gaze upon the temple of the
      Lord.[3]
You whom I revere, gentle and holy ornament to virginity,
Look kindly, O glorious martyr, on the prayers of Damasus, I
      pray.

# AMBROSE

## Introduction

Ambrose, Bishop of Milan from 374–397, was one of the leading churchmen of the fourth century, both as writer and politician. He was born in Trier in the 330s, the son of a high-ranking official who was posted there. He went to Rome to study rhetoric and law and in about 370 he was appointed governor of the area around Milan. Four years later, while he was trying to restore order in the dispute over a successor to Bishop Auxentius of Milan, he was himself chosen as the next bishop, even though he had not actually been baptized yet. Relinquishing his secular career, he gave away his wealth and launched himself on a programme of theological study which included the works of Greek writers such as Basil the Great and Gregory of Nyssa, works which were to influence his own discussions of the faith and through him, those of many western Christians such as Augustine. He soon gained a reputation as an excellent preacher and a man of great goodness (see e.g. Augustine, *Confessions,* 5.13). He took a leading role in the struggle against paganism and against heresy, particularly Arianism which still had powerful support in Milan during his episcopacy. In some ways Ambrose resembles Thomas Becket: both men had an illustrious secular career before attaining enormous power within the Church; both men were involved in the struggle between Church and state, both fighting determinedly for the independence, even superiority of the Church in its relations with the state.

Ambrose's hymns are the only verse works we have by him, but it is clear that they gained enormous popularity immediately and were to be some of the most influential works for the literary and liturgical production of the Middle Ages. There is some dispute as to how many of the hymns in the characteristic form of eight stanzas of four lines of iambic dimeters are genuinely the work of Ambrose: we have contemporary evidence from the pen of Augustine for four of them, namely *Aeterne rerum conditor*, *Deus creator omnium*, *Iam surgit hora tertia*, and *Intende qui regis Israel*, and there are good arguments for accepting that a number of others, such as the *Splendor paternae gloriae* and the Agnes hymn, are also genuine. As to the reasons for composing them, Augustine and Paulinus of Milan,[1] the author of a biography of Ambrose commissioned by Augustine, inform us that some of the hymns were introduced into the liturgy at Milan in 386 at the time of the clash between Arians and Catholics in Milan. Ambrose and the Catholic Christians were being persecuted by Justina, the mother of the boy emperor Valentinian, and their Arian supporters. Ambrose and his people staged a sit-in in their church which Justina wanted to hand over to the Arians. According to Augustine:

> It was then that the practice of singing hymns and psalms was introduced, in keeping with the usage of the Eastern churches, to revive the flagging spirits of the people during their long and cheerless watch. Ever since then the custom has been retained, and the example of Milan has been fol-lowed in many other places, in fact in almost every church throughout the world.

The use of hymns by the whole congregation seems to have been an innovation. No doubt the subjects of Ambrose's hymns were also intended to be influential, for it is clear that he is concerned to stress orthodox Trinitarian, as opposed to Arian, doctrines, as is particularly obvious in the doctrinal statement at the end of *Deus creator omnium* or in *Iam surgit hora tertia* and *Intende qui regis Israel*.[2] Ambrose's hymns with their frequent allusions to baptism and the Eucharist become, as it were, a microcosm of the life of faith.

Like so many of the poets of this period, he also sees the poetic value of the use of allegory and striking metaphors in his hymns, addressing Christ, for example, in terms of the morning light coming to dispel our spiritual somnolence (*Aeterne rerum conditor* lines 29ff.): despite their formal simplicity, Ambrose's hymns are densely packed with powerful images, often drawn from Scripture. Occasionally Ambrose will paraphrase verses from the Psalms or from the New Testament, adapting them to the iambic dimeter: this is particularly striking in the hymn to St John where in five lines Ambrose para-phrases the first three verses of the first chapter of St John's Gospel.

Ambrose's hymn dedicated to Agnes may be compared with the

epitaph by Damasus, and Prudentius' *Peristephanon* 14 on the same subject. If Prudentius' hymn is almost ballad-like in its account of Agnes' clash with the pagan authorities and her willingness to suffer martyrdom, Ambrose's hymns on the martyrs have an almost Horatian compactness and density. Agnes is thought to have died during the Great Persecution of 303–304; although little is known of her life, she soon became the representative of a spiritual ideal uniting chastity with service of Christ.

## Texts

Latin text: ed. A.S. Walpole, *Early Latin Hymns*, Cambridge (1922); ed. J. Fontaine, *Ambroise de Milan: Hymnes*, Paris (1992).

Example of Latin verse form; iambic dimeters

Hymn 8, lines 1–4

Agnes beatae virginis
Natalis est, quo spiritum
Caelo refudit debitum
Pio sacrata sanguine.

## Splendor paternae gloriae

Radiance of the Father's glory
Bringing forth light out of light,
Light of light and source of all light,
Daylight, illuminating days,

True sun, come down upon us,
Shining with brightness eternal,
And pour forth into our minds
The Holy Spirit's brilliance.

Let us pray to the Father, too,
Father of eternal glory,
Father of all-powerful grace,
To rid us of seductive sin

And to fill us with energy,
Blunt the tooth of the envious,

Support us in times of hardship
And give us the grace to endure.

May he guide and control our minds
In bodies pure and full of faith;
May our faith be fervent, burning strong,
Far from the poisons of deceit.

Let our nourishment be Christ,
Let our refreshment be the faith,
Let us with joy drink in the Spirit
Who inebriates us soberly.

May this day be spent joyfully:
May our purity be like the dawn,
May our faith be like the noontide,
May our minds never know the dusk.

As dawn moves steadily on her course
May the Dawn entire advance,
In the Father the Son entire,
In the Word the Father entire.

## Intende qui regis Israel

Hear us, O King of Israel,
Above the cherubim enthroned;
Shine forth upon Ephraim,
Arouse your power and come.[3]

Come redeemer of the peoples,[4]
Show to us the Virgin Birth,
That the entire world may marvel
At such a birth, worthy of God.

Not from a man's seed
But by the Spirit's mystic breath
The Word of God was made flesh
And the fruit of her womb blossomed.

While the Virgin's stomach swells
The gates of chastity are closed,

The banner of her virtues shines:
She is the temple where God resides.

Let him come forth from his room
Which is chastity's royal hall,
A hero of twofold nature,
He is keen to run his course.

From the Father he goes out,
To the Father he returns,
Down to hell he first descends,
Then to the seat of God ascends.

Equal to the eternal Father,
Gird on the trophy of the flesh,
Strengthening with enduring power
Our bodily infirmity.

Already your manger shines out,
The darkness emits a new light:
May this light no night destroy,
May it shine out with constant faith.

## Agnes beatae virginis

Today marks the anniversary
Of the blessed virgin, Agnes,
When she returned her life to heaven,
Sanctified by her pious blood.

For martyrdom she was then ripe
Although for marriage not yet ripe,
While adults faltered in their faith
And the old man, grown weak, gave in.

Her parents, terrified, strengthened
The bolts guarding her chastity,
But faith which cannot be contained
Broke down the doors, imprisoning her.

One might think her about to wed,
So joyful she looked when led forth,

Bringing her husband strange treasure,
Giving her blood as her dowry.

Forced to burn offerings with torches
At the altar of a god she hates,
Her response is: 'Virgins of Christ
Will not touch torches for such use.

This fire will put out the faith,
This flame deprives us of the light.
Here, strike me here! So that I may
Put out this fire with streams of blood.'

With what dignity she bears the wounds!
Covering herself completely with her robes
She takes care that no one should see
Her in her modesty unclothed.

In death her modesty lives on:
Covering her face with her hands,
Collapsing on to bended knees,
Falling to the ground with modesty.

# AUGUSTINE

## Introduction

Only a brief account of Augustine's life and works can be given here, in connection with the translation of excerpts from the only verse work we have of his, the *Psalm against the Donatists*. Augustine was born in Thagaste in Numidia in 354 and died at Hippo, also in North Africa, in 430. Between those dates he also spent time studying at Madaura and Carthage, and then working as a teacher of rhetoric in Thagaste, Carthage and Rome, before gaining a post as professor of rhetoric at Milan in 385. This was where his conversion to a life of Christian asceticism and study finally took place, as recorded in Book 8 of his *Confessions*, and at Easter 387 he was baptized by Ambrose, Bishop of Milan. Returning to North Africa he first lived in his home town of Thagaste, but in 391 he was made a priest at Hippo and it was there that he became bishop in 395, a post he held for the rest of his life, combining the busy life of a bishop with life in an ascetic community where he found time to write a large number of works: letters, sermons, theological and philosophical works, scriptural commentaries, autobiography, most of which have been profoundly influential for the development of Western thought. Much of his time as bishop was devoted to dealing with the various heresies and schisms which were tearing the Church apart at the time: many of his writings are directed against the teachings of the Arians, Manichees, Pelagians and Donatists and it was in his struggle against them that many of his doctrines were hammered out – doctrines on the Church, on grace and free will, on the origin of evil and original sin, and on social theory.

The Donatist controversy erupted in North Africa in the fourth century after a group of Christians there, who were to attract many supporters, claimed that Bishop Caecilian of Carthage had been guilty of collaborating with the authorities during the terrible persecutions in the first decade of the century: this, they believed, compromised the purity of the Church and they therefore rejected any priest whose ordination they considered was tainted by what they regarded as a betrayal of the faith. Augustine, however, held a less rigid view of the Church, a view whereby outside influences and human weaknesses could find a place within the Church. He came to believe that the unity of the Church was more important than its purity and that the purity of the sacraments did not depend on the purity of the priest who administered them because they are given by Christ. Admittedly the Donatists were angered by his appropriation of the concepts of unity and peace which they claimed also to be striving for. Augustine wrote a number of works arguing against Donatist beliefs, including a work on baptism and one on the unity of the Church, during the last decade of the fourth and the first decade of the fifth century. It may have been already in 393, when he was a priest at Hippo, that he composed his *Psalm against the Donatists* which according to his later work, the *Retractions*,[1] he decided to write so as to make the facts known to the ordinary people of his congregation. He chose the form of a song in which each section begins with a letter of the alphabet in sequence from A–V, with a one-line refrain repeated between sections. The song is not written in metrical verse but in a simpler form of sixteen-syllable lines with a break after the eighth syllable and end rhyme, for each line ends in -e. It was Augustine's intention also to avoid unusual vocabulary that the congregation might find difficult. In this 288-line song Augustine begins by stating that the Church is like a net which collects fishes from the sea of this world, scooping up both good and bad until the end of time when the fishes will be separated out: until that time the Church must accept all kinds of people. In connection with this belief he introduces the illustration which was often to recur in his writings, taken from Christ's parable of the wheat and the tares: on the threshing-floor of this world there will be both wheat and tares[2] until such a time as Christ comes to winnow and separate them at the Last Judgement. Augustine stresses the importance of unity and implies that the Donatists, if they truly had Christian love, would not allow a schism to develop. He also manages to give a summary of the history of the Donatist controversy and the song ends with an epilogue in which Mother Church addresses the people, lamenting the fact that they are deserting her.

## Text

Latin text: PL 43, CSEL 51 (1908); ((ed.) H. Vroom, *Le psaume abécédaire de Saint Augustin et la poésie rythmique*, Nijmegen, 1936).

Example of Latin verse form

Lines 1–5

*Omnes qui gaudetis de pace, modo verum iudicate.*
Abundantia peccatorum solet fratres conturbare.
Propter hoc dominus noster voluit nos praemonere
Comparans regnum caelorum reticulo misso in mare
Congreganti multos pisces omne genus hinc et inde.

## Psalm against the Donatists 1–27

*All those of you who rejoice in peace, now it is time to judge the truth.*
A The abundance of sins tends to throw Christians into confusion.
As a result of this our Lord wanted to give us a warning,
Comparing the kingdom of heaven to a net cast into the sea
Which catches up many fishes of every kind from different places.
When they have been pulled to the shore, the fishermen separate them,
Placing the good ones in barrels, the bad they put back in the sea.
Anyone who knows the gospel will recognize these words and tremble.
He sees that the nets are the church, he sees that this world is the sea;
10 The different kinds of fishes are the just mixed up with the sinners;
The shore is the end of the world: then is the time for separation.
Those fish which once burst through the nets were all too attached to the sea.
The barrels are where the saints live, places the sinners cannot reach.

*All those of you who rejoice in peace, now it is time to judge the truth.*

**B** An attentive listener will perhaps ask who has broken
    through this net.

It is those of excessive pride, those who assert their own
    righteousness.

Thus they have caused the schism, setting one altar against
    another,

Handing themselves to the devil when they fight about
    'tradition'

And wish to lay the blame on others for the sin they have
    committed.

20   They have handed over their books and yet they dare to accuse
    us,

Thereby committing a worse crime than that they committed
    before.

Perhaps they can excuse the charge about the books on grounds
    of fear

For did not Peter deny Christ when he was terrified of death?

But how will they rebut the charge of setting altar against altar,

Tearing the peace of Christ apart, and putting all their trust in
    man?

They themselves achieved in peacetime what persecution failed
    to do.

*All those of you who rejoice in peace, now it is time to judge the truth.*

## 170–194

**O** Everyone who knows the Scriptures knows well what I wish
    to make clear.

John the Baptist said quite clearly to the Jews living at that
    time,

That Christ was able to winnow them as if they were his
    threshing floor.[3]

Christ sent out his disciples to preach like workers to the
    harvest:

It was they who gathered in the crop to be winnowed by the
    cross.

Then the righteous devoutly filled the churches, like wheat
    stored in barns;

They sold all that they possessed and said farewell to the
    worldly life;

They were just like the seed which is scattered all over the
    whole earth
So that another crop might spring up to be winnowed at the
    end.
This crop grows up amidst the weeds for there are heretics
    everywhere:
180 The unjust represent the chaff since they are not in unity.[4]
If Macarius[5] was one of these, why do you wish to rebaptize us?

*All those of you who rejoice in peace, now it is time to judge the truth.*
**P** So that you may see my meaning, suppose there are two
    threshing floors.
Undoubtedly in days gone by there were holy men as Scripture
    tells,
For God stated that he left behind seven thousand men in
    safety[6]
And there are many priests and kings who are righteous under
    the law.
There you find so many prophets and many of the people, too.
Tell me which of the righteous at that time claimed an altar for
    himself?
That wicked nation perpetrated a very large number of crimes,
190 They sacrificed to idols and many prophets were put to death,
Yet not a single one of the righteous withdrew from unity.
The righteous endured the unrighteous while waiting for the
    winnower:
They all mingled in one temple but were not mingled in their
    hearts;
They said such things against them and yet they had a single
    altar.

*All those of you who rejoice in peace, now it is time to judge the truth.*

## 259–288 (Epilogue)

Listen, brothers, to what I say and do not be angry with me.
260 For you can reflect upon the fact that what you hear is not false.
What if Mother Church herself were to address you peacefully
And say to you, 'O my sons, why do you complain about your
    mother?
I want to hear from you now the reason why you have deserted
    me.

You make accusations against your brothers: this hurts me
    deeply.
When the pagans were oppressing me, I endured much with
    sorrow,
Many people deserted me but they did so because of fear.
But no one is forcing you to rebel against me in this way.
You say that you are on my side but you must see that this is
    false.
I am called the "catholic" church but you are on Donatus' side.
270 The Apostle Paul ordered me to pray for the kings of this
    world.[7]
You are jealous because the kings now belong to the Christian
    faith.
If you are my sons, why are you jealous that my prayers have
    been heard?
For when they sent presents, you were not willing to accept
    them:
You had forgotten the prophets who long ago predicted this,
Namely that the great kings of the nations would send gifts to
    the church.[8]
When you rejected these gifts, you proved that you were not
    the church
And you have driven Macarius to avenge his suffering.
But I, what have I done to you, I your universal mother?
If I can, I expel the bad; if not, I am forced to bear them.
280 I endure them till they are healed or separated at the end.
Why have you sent me away; why am I tormented by your
    death?
If you greatly hate the wicked, look at those who belong to you.
If you tolerate the wicked, why not do so in unity,
Where no one rebaptizes, no altar stands against another?
You tolerate such wicked ones but without any good reward,
Since what you ought to bear for Christ, you do it for Donatus'
    sake.'
We have sung to you of peace, my brothers, if you will only
    listen.
Our judge is going to come: it is we who give, while he
    demands.

# PAULINUS OF NOLA

## Introduction

Paulinus, who was almost an exact contemporary of Augustine of Hippo, became Bishop of Nola in Campania in 409: he had moved to this small town in 395, having become familiar with it while he had held a government position in the area. He was, however, born in Bordeaux in 353 to a senatorial family of great wealth which he dramatically renounced at the time of his baptism in 389: for this renunciation he was much admired by his Christian contemporaries. He moved to Spain with his wife and then a few years later decided to settle for the rest of his life at Nola, near the shrine of St Felix. Here he lived a life of Christian devotion and chastity, having founded monastic residences for men and women, until his death in 431.

As a young man he had had a good education in Bordeaux, studying with the poet Ausonius whom he regarded as his friend and mentor. When he dedicated himself to a strict Christian life he renounced not only his wealth but also the poetic principles for which Ausonius stood, for he felt they were incompatible with his new convictions: this he makes clear in Poems 10 and 11. He did not, however, cease to practise his poetic skills: he has left us thirty poems as well as about fifty letters, written to such addressees as Augustine, Jerome and Sulpicius Severus (the author of the famous *Life of St Martin*): these letters are among the most beautifully written in Latin from any period from Antiquity to the Renaissance. Of the poems, mostly in hexameters,[1] three are short Psalm paraphrases, two are addressed to Ausonius, defending himself against the charge of neglecting their friendship, one is a consolation poem, one an epithalamium, two (15 and 16) give an account of the life of St Felix and fourteen (known as *Natalicia* or birthday poems) are dedicated to St Felix on the anniversary of the saint's feast day (14 January) each year.

Like Prudentius, Paulinus often goes on at too great length but on the whole his poems, like his letters, are full of a radiant simplicity and warm devotion to Christ, beautiful images and frequent biblical allusions.

I have chosen to translate the shorter of Paulinus' two poems to Ausonius (11), written in hexameters and alternating iambic trimeters and dimeters: as well as these two verse letters from Paulinus, we also have seven letters from Ausonius to Paulinus. Poem 11 is a reply to Ausonius' *Letter* 27, written in 394, in which Paulinus responds to Ausonius' criticisms: in it Paulinus clearly and movingly states his belief that Christian friendship does not depend on physical proximity but on spiritual love which will survive not only separation but also death.[2]

Two excerpts are also translated from one of the *Natalicia* (Poem 20,[3] the birthday poem for the year 406, which runs to 444 lines in its entirety) which starts with an interesting statement of Christian poetic theory and a sort of musical history of salvation, and then gives an amusing account of three miracles involving farm animals selected for slaughter in fulfilment of vows to St Felix, set deep in the Campanian countryside: the story of the pig is given here. I have also translated the opening section of Poem 23, another birthday poem for Felix (written in the year 401), also in hexameters, with its description of spring awakening birdsong and acting as a stimulus to Paulinus' poetry, and two passages from the long consolation in elegiac couplets on the death of the little boy Celsus,[4] the son of Paulinus' friends Pneumatius and Fidelis, whom he assures that they will be reunited with their dead child if they learn to live for Christ.

## Texts

Latin text: CSEL 29 (letters), CSEL 30 (1894) (poems; translated by P.G. Walsh in ACW 40, 1975).

Example of Latin verse form; iambics

Poem 11.49–56

Ego te per omne quod datum mortalibus
    Et destinatum saeculum est,
Claudenti donec continebor corpore,
    Discernar orbe quolibet,
Nec ab orbe longe nec remotum lumine

Tenebo fibris insitum,
Videbo corde, mente conplectar pia
Ubique praesentem mihi.

Elegiac couplets

Poem 31.1–6

Ante puer patribus claris et nomine avito
    Celsus erat, sed nunc celsus agit merito,
Quem dominus tanto cumulavit munere Christus,
    Ut rudis ille annis et novus iret aquis,
Atque bis infantem spatio aevi et fonte lavacri
    Congeminata deo gratia proveheret.

## Poem 11

*Paulinus to Ausonius*

You say that you endure the unbroken silence of my tongue
While you are never silent and you accuse me of living
A life of idleness in hiding: in addition you add the charge
Of neglected friendship and you accuse me of being afraid
Of my wife and punch me hard in the stomach with your verse.
Cease, I pray, to torture one who is yours, and do not seek
To mix bitter words with those of a father, like gall with honey.
My concern has always been, and remains, to honour you
With every act of kindness and to respect you in loyal affection.
10   For me your grace has never been stained
Even by the slightest blemish: I have always feared to offend
        you
Even by a look, or to wound by means of a careless expression.
When I respectfully approached you I composed my looks
Carefully and made my face shine with radiant joy: I did not
        wish
A cloud to gather over my father as a result of my silence.
Following this example my family respected you and still does
        so
And we agree as much in our love for you
As we do in our worship of Christ, in which we are united.
20   What ill-will towards your friends, I ask, has darkened your
        thoughts?

What has caused this rumour to penetrate your ears and reach
    your affection,
Affecting your mind and causing new wounds to afflict
My long-standing loyalty, my love which has been tried and
    tested,
Thus injuring with harmful words a parent loved by his
    children?
My heart cannot be anything but genuine and sincere
And my dutiful affection for such a cultivated father rejects all
These unjust accusations and will not put up with being
    censured falsely,
Innocent as I am: it is hurt more deeply by an unjust wound
For it is as sensitive to offence as it is free from blame.
30   You complain that I have thrown off the yoke joining me to
    you
In our learned studies, but I claim that I have never
Even borne this yoke for only equals can bear a yoke together:
No one joins the strong to the weak and bridles do not sit
    straight
If the team that is pulled together is not of equal strength.
If you join a calf to a bull or a horse to an ass,
If you pair coots with swans and a nightingale with an owl,
Think hazels equal to chestnuts or the wayfaring tree to the
    cypress,[5]
Then you can compare me with you. But Cicero and Virgil
    could hardly bear
An equal yoke with you. Only if I am yoked in love
40   Will I dare to boast that I am your equal
For this allows the lesser to be on equal terms with the greater.
Delightful is the friendship between us with a bond that is
    everlasting
And equal because the laws of mutual love always remain equal.
No foolish rumour has removed this yoke from our necks,
No lengthy separation in far off lands has sundered it,
Nor will it break, even if the whole world and all time keep us
    apart.
Never will I be spiritually separated from you: life itself will
    withdraw
From my body before your face withdraws from my heart.
Throughout the whole of life marked out
50   And granted to mortals,
As long as I am held within this body's confines,

Whatever area of the world divides us,
I will hold you, not far removed from where I am
But engrafted deep within me.
I shall see you in my heart, in my mind embrace you,
You who are with me everywhere.
And when I am freed from the prison of the body
And from this earth I can fly forth,
Wherever I am placed by our Father, yours and mine,
60  There, too, I will hold you in my soul.
In fact the same end will not detach me
From my body and from my love for you,
For since my soul survives when my limbs dissolve
And continues to exist, being of heavenly origin,
It must of course retain both its senses and feelings
Just as it retains its own life, too;
And as it is unable to die, so it cannot forget
But will continue to live, remembering you for ever.


## Poem 23.1–44

Spring sees the onset of birdsong and my tongue has its own
    spring, too,
The birthday of Felix, and when that day dawns winter itself
    flowers
And the crowds rejoice; even though it is still a time
Of darkness and cold spent in winter quarters covered in frost,
A time of year when the earth is frozen and white,
When that day comes, our devotion and delight create a joyful
Spring. Cares are banished from the breast and sorrow,
The winter of the soul, departs; the heart is bright,
All clouds of sadness dispelled. Just as the gentle swallow
10  Recognizes mild days, as does the white bird with black wings
And that turtle dove, related to the devoted dove,
And only at the onset of spring do the copses ring with the
    finch[6]
And with those that flit silently beneath the rough hedges,
Soon everywhere the birds rejoice at the return of spring
With songs as various as their colourful wings:
In the same way I, too, recognize this day which every year
Is celebrated anew in due honour of the excellent Felix.
Now peaceful spring is reborn for me as the year rejoices,
Now it is pleasing to open my mouth in poetry, to offer songs

20   In fulfilment of our vows and to celebrate spring with new
      voice.
O Christ my God, flow into my heart, quench my thirst from
      heavenly springs:
Even a drop from you sprinkled on me deep within
Will be a stream. Is it surprising if you fill the smallest soul
With a tiny drop of dew, you who were made man
In a small body but filled the world with seed eternal
And saved the whole earth with a single drop of blood?
Look upon me with kindness, source of the Word, God the Word,
And make me like that bird in springtime, vocal with its lovely
      song,
That hides beneath the verdant hedges and with various tunes
30   Soothes the depths of the countryside, using its single tongue
To pour forth no single sound, varying its song:
A bird with feathers of one colour but with a rich tapestry of
      sound.
One moment it produces smooth melodies, the next moment
Long and piercing sounds, and then it starts upon an almost
Plaintive song; then suddenly cutting short its plaint
It frustrates the astonished listener by breaking off its song.[7]
But may your grace, O Christ, flow upon me without ceasing.
And yet I beg that it be granted to me, as to that bird,
That I might vary my song and produce
40   Each year the promised songs with different utterances
Though from a single mouth, for grace in its abundance always
      provides
Different subjects through the marvellous powers of the Lord
Which Christ our God supplies in large measure in our beloved
      Felix,
Performing clear marvels by means of miracles which bring
      salvation.

## Poem 20.28–61

The subject of my poem is no fiction, though I use the poetic
      art:
I will tell of things that happened, reliably, without a poet's
      deceit,
30   For far be it from a servant of Christ to utter lies.
May such techniques delight the pagans as they worship what
      is false

But our only skill is our faith, our only music Christ
Who showed that a wonderful concord of unbalanced harmony
Was of old achieved in himself, a harmony he bestowed on one
    body
When he assumed human nature, he who combined
The life-giving God with virtue infused, uniting two in
    himself
And bringing completely separate natures into one.
So that man might become a god, God was made man by
    himself
For he is God, son of God the Father, who owes it not to grace
40    But to nature that he is sole heir of the Father Almighty,
Alone possessing as his own what he presents as a gift
To those to whom kindly faith has granted a heavenly reward.
He then is truly our poetic inspiration,
He is the true David who restored the lyre of this body
Which had lain for long, its frame decaying;
Taking up the silent instrument, its strings broken
By original sin, the Lord repaired it for his own use
And when mortals had been joined with God
He restored the whole world to its original form
50    So that all things might be new, and the dust removed from
    them.
God himself was the master intending to restore this lyre
And he himself hung his lyre upon the tree of wood,
To repair it by means of the cross which destroyed the sin of the
    flesh.
Thus he constructed from a variety of peoples
A single human lyre tuned to the melody of heaven,
Fixing together all kinds of people into one body.
Then when the strings were plucked with the plectrum of the
    Word,
The sound of the Gospel instrument filled the whole world
With praise of God; Christ's golden lyre echoed throughout the
    world,
60    Producing one melody out of innumerable tongues,
While the new songs respond to God with matching strings.


## 312–387

A group of farmers some way away from here,
Who tilled Apulian land beyond the city of Benevento,

Selected from their large litter of bristly pigs
One which still nuzzled with its soft snout at the milky teats;
For a long time they tended the pig and fed it up
As an offering and when it was ready they set off
To lead it to the church consecrated to St Felix
So that after slaughtering its huge body could feed
320 A great number of the hungry which would please the martyr.
But the pig, weighed down by more fat than its legs could bear,
Was unable to raise itself up for long and at the very beginning
Of the journey it collapsed, unable to move from that spot:
No shouts or slaps or whips could make it. The owners,
    heartbroken,
Left it lying there, entrusting to their friends what they were
    forced
To abandon. Their troubled minds wavered, hesitating:
They did not want to cancel the journey they had vowed to make,
But to make the long journey empty-handed to Felix's
    venerable shine
Without the gift they had promised would be embarrassing.
330 And so, filled with uncertainty, they at last decided
That they would choose for their offering the same number
Of choice piglets from the same litter as the number of years
    attained
By that pig that remained immobile, oppressed by its own
    weight.
Their faith and devotion, eager to perform in haste
The obligations of their vow, reckoned in this way:
A number of smaller animals would make up for a single
    plump one.
And so they came here to the holy shrine and having fulfilled
    their vows
They returned to their lodging some distance away.
For at the time it happened that the houses round the martyr's
    church
340 Were filled with great crowds of people pouring in.
As a result they were content to stay in a remote cottage,
Far from here, tucked away deep in the country, where next
    morning
They prepared to set out on the return journey as soon as
    blushing dawn
Brought forth the day. The cottage door opens and out from the
    hut

Comes the visitor: the man catches sight of the pig he knows so
    well
Standing there in front of the door, miraculously ready:
It appears to be telling its master that it was sent
And it licks its master's feet as if it wants to greet him.
The man is overjoyed. The pig grunts in a friendly way,
    behaving like
350  A loving child, and snuffling with its twitching snout
It kisses him, as if it knows it is the offering its master owes.
It rushes forward, inviting to its throat the knife that is slow in
    coming;
Under whose guidance, I ask you, did it manage to find its way
In unknown territory, how did it get the feet to enable it to run
    so far,
That animal which at the start of the journey did not have the
    strength
To move a short distance, weighed down by the mass of flabby
    fat?
There was certainly no hand leading such a huge beast on the
    long road
Nor was it carried, nor did its own ideas compel it
To make its way so far on a long journey through an unknown
    area.
360  For even in the case of people of keen intelligence
Who have been given clear directions through foreign places,
If they lack a leader to show them the way,
Then blind error causes them to go astray in unfamiliar parts.
Who then guided this pig? Where did it get the will
To follow its masters? Or the perception which made it realize
That its long life had prepared it as a votive offering?
Where did the animal get this determination such as rarely
Stirs even the faithful? It was as if the pig, having stayed
    behind
Out of laziness, became aware of its guilt and was struck by
    pious fear;
370  By coming it wished to expiate the fault it had incurred by
    staying,
Thereby compensating for the sin of idle sloth
And even though rather late in the day, it obediently joined
Its masters. This is clearly an extraordinary sign,
Which heavenly authority granted by means of the pig's bold
    deed

In going alone on a long journey; such an intelligent pig,
Directing its steps unswervingly through unknown territory!
What about this extraordinary fact, too? The fact that
On its way here to the area beyond Benevento
(Whether it boldly trotted along the public highway
380   Without meeting any crowds anywhere along the way
Or whether it made its way through remote woodland)
No hand attacked it with weapons, no wild beast with its bite.
What hand guided it or protected it on its lonely journey?
It must obviously have been concealed by some mist, remaining
        unseen
Or it was snatched up in the air and arrived by wind rather
        than on foot,
Suddenly gliding down from the sky to its master's lodgings
Where the four-footed visitor stopped before the unfamiliar
        door.


## Poem 31.1–46

Until recently Celsus was a boy with illustrious ancestors
And a famous family, but now he has won the right to live *in
        excelsis*,
For Christ our Lord has granted him the great privilege
Of entering the water although as yet but a new recruit;
Grace repeated twice brought the child to God,
First in the waters of baptism and then at the end of his life.
Alas, what am I to do? I am troubled by my affection, uncertain
Whether I ought to rejoice or grieve: the boy deserves both.
My love for him drives me to tears but also to joy
10   For my faith bids me rejoice, my affection bids me weep.
I weep for him who was lent to us for such a short time,
Such a small profit to his parents for such a lovely treasure.
Then when I consider the undying benefits of eternal life
Which God prepares in heaven for the innocent,
I am glad he has died after living only a short time
So that he might quickly enjoy the riches of heaven
And not be in contact for long with earthly things
In the body's fragile lodging through association with the
        wicked;
Instead unstained by any sin that the world might give
20   He might more worthily go forward to the eternal Lord.
And so this child, owed to God rather than to us,

And yet also pleasing to God for our sakes,
This little one had entered upon his eighth year
And was enjoying his early life as it raced swiftly by.
Already he bore the yoke of boyhood on his tender shoulders,
Subject to the harsh rule of the grammar master;
But whatever the boy was taught, to his master's amazement
This noble child absorbed it all for his mind was quick to learn.
His parents were pleased but their hearts trembled with
    foreboding
30  As they feared the envy such a gift might provoke;
And indeed it was not long before Christ our God in heaven
Summoned this dear soul and took it with due honour,
Snatching it suddenly from earth because it was more worthy
To live in close association with the assemblies of the saints.
The cause of death was fluid welling up in his throat
For a large tumour caused his milk-white neck to swell;
When pressure was applied it disappeared but as it vanished, it
    moved
To the internal parts of his body, banishing life from his vital
    organs.
The earth received its share when the body was buried
40  While the spirit departed, carried off in an angel's arms.
His bereaved parents escorted the lifeless corpse
While Celsus lives happily in paradise on high.
You loving parents, I beg you, cease to mourn excessively
In case your devotion should become culpable.
For to mourn a blessed soul is impious piety
And to weep for one who rejoices in God is a destructive love.


## 199–274

Let us dispel complaints and grief from our ungrateful hearts,
200 Let us dry our eyes and allow clear vision to return,
Let us trust to Christ, because in him we see
That we shall rise with the same bodies as those in which we die,
And that we shall be changed and take on angelic form,
Clothed in garments of heavenly splendour.
But if such darkness covers our clouded minds
And our sluggish perceptions are dulled within our feeble
    bodies,
So that because divine matters are hidden from our physical
    sight,

You claim the Scriptures cannot be trusted,
Then let Paul teach that things visible are transient
210 And that things eternal are hidden from human eyes.[8]
You fool, look upon earthly things but believe in heavenly ones;
Contemplate the world with your eyes, God with your mind.
This is the way to gain precious faith; for just as grace is no
 longer
Grace if it is bestowed according to merit,
So too there is no faith apart from that which believes
What it sees not and seeks the eternal with hope as its guide.
Wretched mortals, always complaining, dispense at last
With wicked thoughts, your hearts softened.
Why, I pray, do you still seek after illusions with heavy heart
220 And in your folly love things that are deceptive?
Change your ways, tear apart the chains of death
And voluntarily set your shoulders to a most comfortable yoke.[9]
For the sake of freedom choose the heavenly chains,
Chains which sin can break and love can bind.
If you seek the darkness, you go astray in bright daylight,
And if you see by night, you walk blind by day.
Let us open to Christ the eyes and ears of our soul
So that our minds, closed by sin, may be open to God.
For God reveals his promises to physical sight, too,
230 And already shows his secrets to eyes that see clearly.
All the seeds of the earth and the stars of heaven
Experience this phenomenon of resurrection.
Nights and days, risings and settings alternate:
At night I die, I rise by day.
I sleep, all drowsy in a semblance of physical death,
I am woken from sleep as if from annihilation.
What of the crops, the leaves of the forests, the seasons?
Without doubt all pass away and return according to the same
 laws.
As spring appears again all things take on a new form,
240 Brought back to life after winter's death.
All things beneath the heavens repeatedly experience exactly
 the same
As happens to man, to whom the creatures of the world are
 subject.
But men ask with what body all the dead will be restored
And how man can be created again out of ashes.
If the revelations made by the holy prophets are not enough,

Let mute creation give its guarantee: believe things that are
  obvious.
You see that no seeds sprout in the fields
Unless they die first, dissolved by crumbling decay:[10]
You sow naked seeds, you reap them clothed in fruits;[11]
250 You scatter dry grain, then harvest it, its fruits now multiplied.
What twisted faith, what lack of confidence is ours,
That we should trust the earth but be uncertain about God.
In fact the earth dared not promise me anything
Nor was it able; indeed the fields often cheated me, hardly
  producing
Crops equal to the seed; but despite my disappointment
I do not hesitate to entrust to it my hopes for a harvest
Nor do I weary of putting in all this undoubted effort
For a doubtful harvest, of entrusting bare things to the bare
  soil.
But if the earth can restore the seed decayed
260 Which it does according to the covenant of the everlasting
  Lord,
Do you believe it will be a hard task for the Almighty
To restore us from something, we who were from nothing
  made?
I was nothing but by God's agency I was born, brought into
  being;
Soon I will exist once again from my own particular seed.
For although our bones are reduced to meagre ashes,
This dust contains the seeds of our whole body,
And though the earth empties tombs and absorbs
The ashes mixed with the soil related to them,
Even then the Almighty keeps them intact
270 Though to men's eyes they seem to have faded away.
On that great day we shall see the bodies we now think
Have been destroyed rise in their entirety for God,
For whom no nature perishes, for all that exists anywhere
Is enclosed within the Creator's embrace.

# ENDELECHIUS

## Introduction

Although the identity of the poet whose name is given in the manuscript as Severus Sanctus Endelechius is not known for certain, Paulinus of Nola mentions a friend of his, a rhetor, with the name Endelechius (*Letter* 28.6) and it is possible that this is indeed the author of the poem known as *De Mortibus Boum* (*The Death of the Cattle*). The poem, closely modelled on Virgil's *Eclogues*, and in particular *Eclogue* 1 with its tale of rural suffering and the news of assistance from a god, tells of a plague[1] which devastates vast areas of central and western Europe, finally reaching Gaul where the poem is set. The plague kills many animals whose owners have no way of saving their beasts, until they hear from Tityrus how his cattle were saved by having the sign of the cross made on their foreheads. Confronted with this miracle, the other two countrymen, Bucolus and Aegon, are converted to Christianity: at the end of the poem they abandon the pastoral landscape and set off for the city to go to church. The effectiveness of miracles in converting pagans is very much a theme of the period. This poem of 132 verses in 33 stanzas is unusual in being not about the delights of country life but about suffering, demonstrating the belief that there can be no peace and happiness in this life without God's grace.

## Text

Latin text: PL 19, *Anthologia Latina* I.2 (1906; repr. Amsterdam, 1972), *Hirtengedichte aus spätrömischer und karolingischer Zeit* (ed. D. Korzeniewski, Darmstadt, 1976).

Example of Latin verse form; the metre is the so-called Second Asclepiad, used by Horace in *Odes* 1.6, for example.

Lines 1–4

Quidnam solivagus, Bucole, tristia
Demissis graviter luminibus gemis?
Cur manant lacrimis largifluis genae?
Fac, ut norit amans tui.

## Eclogue

*Aegon*:    Why do you wander alone, Bucolus, sighing
              miserably,
            Your eyes downcast as if you felt oppressed?
            Why do copious tears stream down your cheeks?
            Please explain this to your friend.

5   *Bucolus*:   Aegon, I beg you, let me bury myself
            Deep in silence, painful as my emotions are.
            For he who reveals his troubles reopens the wound;
            Suppressing them in silence allows it to heal.

*Aegon*:    The opposite of what you say is true; your claim is
              false.
10          For a burden shared becomes less heavy
            But what is covered over boils up more fiercely.
            It helps to talk when one is sad.

*Bucolus*:   You are aware, Aegon, what a large flock I possessed,
            And that my animals grazed beside every stream;
15          They filled even the hollow valleys,
            The fields and the mountain ridges.

            Now all hope based on my wealth has been dashed
            And all that my prolonged efforts produced
              throughout
            My life has been lost in the space of two days.
20          So swiftly do troubles advance!

            This dreadful plague is now said to be spreading.
            Not long ago it caused the Pannonians, Illyrians
            And Belgians terrible destruction, and now
            It is attacking us, too, in its foul progress.

25  *Aegon*:    But you used to know of medicinal juices
Which could protect from harmful destruction.
Why do you not forestall the danger you fear
By applying your healing hands?

*Bucolus*:    Such terrors have no clear warning signs;
30            What the disease attacks it also destroys.
It admits no lingering, allows no delay.
Thus death anticipates the plague.

To the wagons I had yoked my strong oxen,
Chosen as carefully as I could;
35            Both of them shared the same thoughts,
And their bells tinkled in harmony,

Both the same age, with the same colour bristles,
They were both gentle, both equally strong
And they had the same fate, for in mid-course
40            The pair of them collapsed in identical death.

I was sowing the seed deep in the softened earth;
The clods were crumbling after all the rain;
The plough moved easily through the furrows,
Nowhere did the ploughshare stick.

45            The ox on the left collapsed suddenly and fell;
It was only the second summer since he was tamed.
At once I unyoked his grieving partner,
Not fearing further misfortune now.

But faster than one could say, death seized him
50            Although he had always been healthy before.
Now his flanks jerked in prolonged spasms,
He lay down his head, all strength gone.

*Aegon*:    I feel anguish and torment, sorrow and grief,
For my heart is shattered by your losses
55            As if they were my own; and yet I believe
Your herd is now safe?

*Bucolus*:    No, wretched as I am, something far worse lay ahead
                of me.
            For it would be some comfort in my trouble, if only
                a little,
            If I had had a subsequent litter to replace
60          What this present plague had taken.

            But who would have believed it? The young animals,
                too,
            Were killed at the same time; I myself saw
            The pregnant cow collapse; I saw two lives
            Destroyed in the one body.

65          Here wanders a heifer on wobbly legs,
            Refusing to drink, neglecting the grass,
            But she cannot get far for she is limping
            And falls heavily, shackled by death.

            Over there is a calf that just now
70          Was leaping and frolicking around,
            Going to suckle his mother; but soon he sucks
            The plague from the diseased udder.

            When his mother, wounded by this sorrowful pain,
            Saw her calf closing his eyes in death,
75          She mooed repeatedly, groaning pitifully
            And collapsed, longing for death.

            Then as if she feared that thirst with parched throat
            Might choke the calf, while she lay there dying too,
            She moved her udder to her calf that was already
                dead.
80          Love remains strong even after death.

            There is the bull, husband and father of the healthy
                herd,
            With his strong neck and broad forehead;
            He was happy and extremely proud of himself
            But even he collapsed in the grassy meadow.

85     As many are the falling leaves of which the trees
       Are stripped when battered by the icy north wind,
       As thickly as the snowflakes flutter in a blizzard,
       So numerous are the cattle which have died.

       Now the whole ground is covered with corpses,
90     Their bodies bloated, their bellies swollen,
       Their eyes are white with livid patches,
       Their legs stiff, their feet stretched out.

       Already baleful flocks of birds, grim vultures,
       Are hovering; already packs of dogs
95     Press round to tear the entrails and feed on them.
       Alas, why not on mine also?

*Aegon*:     Why, I ask you, why is it that death's grim fate
       Is so inconsistent, leaping over some
       But striking others? Look at Tityrus,
100    Happily driving his healthy flock.

*Bucolus*:   Yes, I see him now. Come tell us, Tityrus,
       Which God has saved you from these disasters,
       So that the plague that ravaged your neighbours'
          flocks
       Has not affected yours at all?

105 *Tityrus*:   The sign which is said to represent the cross of God
       Who alone is worshipped in the big cities,
       Christ, the glory of the eternal Godhead
       Whose only Son he is,

       This sign, marked in the centre of the forehead,
110    Brought my cattle's sure salvation.
       And for this reason this powerful God
       Is now truly hailed as our Saviour.

       The raging plague directly fled from the herds.
       The epidemic lost its strength. But if you wish
115    To pray to this God, it is sufficient to believe.
       Faith alone makes your prayer effective.

His altar is not wet with bloody sacrifice,
No slaughter of cattle averts disease,
But simplicity and purity of mind
120     Obtain the desired rewards.

*Bucolus*:   If you are sure about this, Tityrus, I will without
    delay
Begin to perform the rites of the true faith.
I will be glad to flee from the old error,
For it is deceptive and illusory.

125 *Tityrus*:   Already I am keen to hurry and visit
The temple of almighty God; come, Bucolus,
Let us go together – it is not far –
And acknowledge Christ's divinity.

*Aegon*:   Let me join you in your happy plan.
130     For how could I doubt that mankind, too,
Will for ever benefit from this sign
Which overcame the powerful plague.

# PRUDENTIUS

## Introduction

Aurelius Prudentius Clemens was born in Spain in about 348 and died some time after 405. In the 45-line Preface to his collection of poems, written when he was in his fifties, Prudentius gives the reader some information about his life and his motive for writing; most of his life had been spent in a successful career in public administration until near the end of his life he decided to give up his career to devote himself to Christ, a move reminiscent of the dramatic renunciation Paulinus of Nola had decided upon a few years earlier. Prudentius visited Rome on pilgrimage in 402–3 and it was at about this time that he started to write poetry with a passionately Christian bias and in the space of a few years produced eight works. He was clearly determined to produce, even at this late stage of life, something worthwhile to show that his 'sinning soul' had 'put off her foolishness' (Preface 35); he must have sensed that he had poetic talent, in addition to a good grounding in literary studies, and that he should use this talent to praise God and to support the true faith. In the final lines of his Preface he alludes to the works he has presumably already written, works in which he variously fights against heresies, expounds the Catholic faith, attacks the pagan cults and celebrates the martyrs' achievements. To all these works he gives Greek titles, just as Ovid chose a Greek title for his *Metamorphoses*.

The *Cathemerinon* (*The Daily Round*) consists of twelve long hymn-like poems in a variety of metres, the first six of which are written for specific times of day, while of the remainder one is for the festival of Christmas (11), another for Epiphany (12) and one a hymn for the burial of the dead (10). Here we have chosen to translate the ninth hymn, a 'hymn for every hour' which takes the form of a meditation on the life of Christ, a kind of potted history of Christ's life on earth,[1] his death and resurrection which makes it like a condensed version of Juvencus' poem on the Gospels; it is from this hymn that the lines translated in the famous hymn 'Of the Father's love begotten' are taken (lines 10ff.).

The *Apotheosis* (*The Divinity of Christ*, but occasionally referred to as *On the Trinity*) is a poem in 1084 hexameters, preceded by a double preface, in which the poet defends Christian teaching on the divinity of Christ and the equal status of the Father and Son within the Trinity. It is no dry theological treatise but a lively invective against erroneous beliefs, full of fantastic images and lyrical expressions intended to put forward the belief that in Christ human nature has triumphed and that as a result each individual human has the hope that he will share in Christ's resurrection.

In the 966 hexameters, prefaced by 63 iambic trimeters, of the *Hamartigenia* (*The Origin of Sin*) Prudentius investigates the origin of evil, attacking the dualism characteristic of Gnostic and Manichean sects and emphasizing human moral responsibility:[2] this was a tricky area, as Augustine found to his cost, for if one emphasized mankind's moral responsibility and freedom, one could be accused of Pelagianism, but if one went the other way and stressed the need for grace to guide free will, one might fall victim to a charge of Manichean determinism. In this Catch 22 situation Prudentius seems to have managed to avoid being accused of heresy. This poem too is filled with vigorous invective and colourful descriptions, with plentiful references to Old Testament stories but also occasionally to classical mythology, such as 'the fires of Tartarus dark-hued with molten lead'. It contains the famous line 'The hunger for gold only grows keener from the gold it has got' (257), followed by a wonderful attack on luxury and self-indulgence, part of which is translated below.

The two books *Contra Symmachum* (*Against Symmachus*) are based on a clash between pagan and Christian beliefs which occurred in 384 when the pagan Prefect of Rome, Symmachus, appealed to the emperor for permission to restore the Altar of Victory, a powerful pagan symbol, to the Senate house in Rome. Bishop Ambrose of Milan, in a powerful address full of scorn for pagan pretensions, intervened to stop the young emperor acceding to Symmachus' request.[3] The first book of the *Contra Symmachum* (which is preceded by an allegorical preface, as are most of Prudentius' works) consists of a violent attack on the pagan gods, full of ridicule, while in the second book the poet uses Ambrose's arguments to refute Symmachus. Prudentius makes it clear that he is not anti-Rome but believes that

Rome has now been transformed into a Christian capital and in this form its greatness will live on, rejuvenated.

The work entitled *Peristephanon* (*The Martyrs' Crowns*) consists of fourteen hymns in various, mostly Horatian, metres in which the poet celebrates the death and victory of a number of martyrs (mainly Roman and Spanish), most of whom had suffered martyrdom either during the persecutions of the 250s under the emperors Decius and Valerian or during the great persecutions at the beginning of the fourth century under Maximian and Diocletian. Prudentius provides realistic, dramatic accounts of the events surrounding the execution of such saints as Cyprian (13), Lawrence (2) and Agnes (14). The form of the hymns is a kind of blend of epic and lyric, which in some cases resembles a ballad. These vivid descriptions not only inspired devotion to these particular saints at a time when the cult of the saints was becoming part of the life of the Catholic Church, but also inspired the writing of medieval martyr legends, as well as depictions of the saints in medieval and baroque art.

Undoubtedly Prudentius' most famous poem is the so-called *Psychomachia* (*The Battle for* (or *'in'*) *the Soul*), a work of 915 hexameters, prefaced by 68 lines of iambic trimeters. It is arguable that no other poem of Late Antiquity has had such an influence on later literary production, particularly by its use of the personification of vices and virtues.[4] In the preface, an incident in the life of Abraham, taken from Genesis, is interpreted allegorically as symbolizing the battle against vice which must be fought if man's soul is to become a temple to God. If the poet starts with an episode from the first book of the Scriptures, at the end of the poem it is to the final book of Scripture, Revelation, that he makes copious references in the description of the temple built by Concord and Faith when the battle is over. In the poem proper allegory and typology remain dominant in the series of set piece battles between a personified vice and its corresponding virtue (e.g. Anger against Patience, Sensuality against Modesty, etc.) and in the speeches made by the protagonists, which are interspersed with references to certain exemplary biblical figures who proved triumphant over various vices. These battle scenes are described in epic manner, with much explicit violence perpetrated even by the Virtues, a fact which many have found off-putting. However, the manner in which the Virtues and Vices behave and speak is on the whole psychologically realistic and perceptive, and even amusing. Indulgence (Luxuria), for example, is presented as entering the battle still affected by the previous night's feasting: she has no need to use arrows or javelins to overcome the enemy but does so by means of fragrant flowers which she languidly tosses from her lovely chariot, causing those in the Virtues' ranks to grow feeble, drop their weapons and gaze longingly after her until Soberness (Sobrietas) intervenes with biting words. In the case of the clash between Pride and Humility, the proverbial 'Pride comes before a fall' is visually enacted, as after her long speech Pride falls into a hole dug by her ally Deceit. The language Prudentius uses is inevitably influenced by such writers of epic as Virgil, Ovid and Lucan but the poet also derives a number of unusual words from Juvenal. Characteristically there are also a number of neologisms.

One other work of Prudentius remains to be mentioned: the *Dittochaeon* (possibly meaning *Twofold Nourishment*) in 196 hexameters, divided into verses of four lines, each verse summarizing some episode derived from the Old Testament or the New. It has been suggested that these forty-nine verses were designed to accompany paintings. This work is not referred to in the Preface to Prudentius' works.

The fact that Prudentius has been called the 'Horace and Virgil of the Christians', because he uses Horatian and Virgilian metres and writes epic, has made his poetry more legitimate to classicists than that of any other Christian Latin poet, but this is not enough to make him 'the greatest Christian poet of antiquity'. His work is of interest not only because of the classical connections, but for the rich poetic language he creates, for the cultural content and the new psychological interests he introduces, for the relation between pagan and Christian elements and for the way he points forward to the concerns and literary forms of the Middle Ages. It is true that at its best his poetry is often moving and often colourful, but at times it must be admitted that it verges on the overblown, the long-winded and grotesque.

Below is translated, first of all, part of the *Hamartigenia*, in which Prudentius describes how we use our bodily senses wrongly, for purposes of self-indulgence. His tone here is as so often satirical. Second, the entire ninth poem of the *Cathemerinon* is translated, praising Christ and giving a list of his miracles, each one summed up in three lines. Third comes an excerpt from the *Psychomachia* in which Avarice's behaviour on the battlefield is described: this long passage includes Avarice's speech and that of Generosity, the virtue that attacks and subdues her. This clash is the final one in the battle between the Vices and the Virtues: the rest of the poem tells how Concord and Faith lay the foundations for the temple of the soul. Finally, the whole of *Peristephanon 3* is included, telling the story of the martyr Eulalia, a young girl who like Agnes is thought to have died in the persecutions of Diocletian. Eulalia refused to sacrifice to the gods, and is burnt alive as a punishment.

Eulalia also appears in a sermon attributed to Augustine (published by G. Morin in *Revue Bénédictine* 8 (1891)), in a poem (8.4) by Venantius Fortunatus, in Gregory of Tours' *De Gloria Martyrum* and in the oldest surviving French poem, the *Cantilène de sainte Eulalie*.

## Texts

Latin text: CSEL 61 (1926), PL 59–60, CCL 126 (1926), Loeb Classical Library (1949–53), Budé edition, Paris (1943–51).

Example of Latin verse forms: hexameters

*Hamartigenia* 389–397

His aegras animas morborum pestibus urget
Praedo potens, tacitis quem viribus interfusum
Corda bibunt hominum; serit ille medullitus omnes
Nequitias spargitque suos per membra ministros.
Namque illic numerosa cohors sub principe tali
Militat horrendisque animas circumsidet armis,
Ira, Superstitio, Maeror, Discordia, Luctus,
Sanguinis atra Sitis, Vini Sitis et Sitis Auri,
Livor, Adulterium, Dolus, Obtrectatio, Furtum.

*Cathemerinon* 9.1–3; trochaic tetrameters catalectic

Da, puer, plectrum, choreis ut canam fidelibus
Dulce carmen et melodum, gesta Christi insignia.
Hunc Camena nostra solum pangat, hunc laudet lyra.

*Cathemerinon* 8.1–4; sapphics

Christe, servorum regimen tuorum,
Mollibus qui nos moderans habenis
Leniter frenas, facilique saeptos
    Lege coerces . . .

*Peristephanon* 3.1–5; dactylic trimeter hypercatalectic

Germine nobilis Eulalia
Mortis et indole nobilior
Emeritam sacra virgo suam

Cuius ab ubere progenita est
Ossibus ornat, amore colit.

## Hamartigenia 298–353

Indulgence controls all the animating forces of our life
Which our Creator made and established in our five senses.
300 For the ears and eyes, for the nostrils and the palate
We seek experiences tainted by vicious practices;
Even touch itself which operates throughout the body
Solicits tender stroking and seductive caresses.
Alas that nature's innate laws should have collapsed
And her gifts been dragged away, captive, while lust prevails.
Every power is perverted, for whatever the Almighty gave
Men to possess, they turn to its opposite use.
Is that the reason, I ask, why the watchful eye is set beneath
The soft eyelid, so that it can stare at the effeminate dancers'
310 Shameful bodies whirling around in the theatre,
Polluting its wretched vision with filthy amusements?
Is this why we breathe through those holes linked together
Through the two nostrils leading down from the centre of the
        brain,
So that ill-gotten pleasure might drink in the attractions
Offered by a shameless whore with perfumed hair?
Was it for the idle melodies produced by a lyre-playing girl,
For the sound of strings, the indecent party songs
Which inflame desire, that God gave us ears, spread open wide,
And ordained that the voice should travel and penetrate
320 Their cavernous passages? Does the sense of taste set in the
        moist mouth
Exist for this reason, that spiced dishes might entice
The glutton's jaded appetite and stimulate his palate,
And so that he may prolong his feasting into the night
With numerous courses, exhausting his belly heavy with
        excess?
Whether something is hard or soft, whether rough or smooth,
Whether it is hot or cold to the touch, God wanted us to learn
Through the medium of the sense of touch.
But we keep our skin smooth by spreading luxurious duvets
and linen sheets and lying on a couch which makes us delicate.
330 Happy is he who can use with moderation the gifts
Granted to him and maintain frugal limits in enjoying them,

He whom the world's gorgeous display and lovely charms,
Its deceptive riches filled with glittering attractions
Do not seduce, as they do a child, or enslave to a foolish
    passion;
Happy is he who detects the deadly poison beneath the false
    delights,
Concealed beneath something that is not really good.
But in earlier times this was both good and holy for us,
In the beginning of things when Christ created the world.
For God saw that it was good, as Moses himself,
340 The historian of the world's birth, testified when he said,
'God saw that all that he had created was good.'[5]
This I will follow, this I will hold firmly in my mind,
That by God's inspiration the holy prophet,
Recounting the beginnings of light in days long past,
    proclaimed
That whatever God and Wisdom made was good.
The creator of good, then, is the Father and with the Father,
    Christ,
For He is God and God the Father and the Son are one,
Seeing that nature makes them one for they both have
A single will, authority, power and love.
350 Yet they are not for that reason two gods or two creators
Of the world, since there is no difference in kind,
No separation in their sphere of work, none in their mind:
A single creator brought forth all things good.

## Cathemerinon 9

Give me my plectrum, boy, that I may sing in faithful verse
A sweet and melodious song, of the glorious deeds of Christ.
Him alone may my Muse sing of, Him alone may my lyre
    praise.
Christ it is whose future coming was proclaimed by the priest-
    king[6]
In his vestments, with voice, with strings and percussion,
Drinking deep the spirit flowing into him from heaven.
We sing of miracles performed and already proved.
The world is witness and the earth denies not what it has
    seen,
That God was made manifest to men to teach them in person.
10 Of the Father's love begotten before the beginning of the world,

Called Alpha and Omega, himself both source and end
Of all that is, has been, and will exist in times to come.
He commanded and they were created, he spoke and they were
　　made,
Earth, heavens, the depths of the sea — the triple structure of
　　the universe —
And all that inhabits them beneath the lofty orbs of sun and
　　moon.
He put on a mortal body's form and limbs vulnerable to death,
To prevent the destruction of the race sprung from the first
　　creature
Whom a deadly law had plunged deep into hell.
O what a blessed birth was then, when a virgin in labour,
20　Having conceived by the Holy Spirit, brought forth our
　　salvation,
And the child who is the world's redeemer revealed his sacred
　　face.
Let the heights of heaven sing, all you angels, sing,
Let all the powers everywhere sing in praise of God,
Let no tongue be silent, let every voice ring in harmony.
Look how the one who was foretold by seers in ages past
And pledged in the prophets' reliable writings,
Shines forth, he who was promised long ago: let all things
　　praise him.
The water poured into the jars turns into classy Falernian
　　wine;[7]
The servant announces that wine has been drawn from the
　　water-jar,
30　The master himself is astounded at the taste when the cups are
　　dipped in.
'I order that diseased and ulcerous limbs and rotting flesh
Must be washed,' he said; his orders are carried out
And the cleansing of the wounds purifies the swollen skin.[8]
Eyes that are buried in perpetual darkness you smear
With wholesome mud and the nectar of your sacred mouth:
At once this cure causes the light to return to the eyes that are
　　open now.[9]
You rebuke the raging wind for turning the seas upside down
From its very depths, with its dark storms, and tossing the ship
　　off course:
The wind obeys your commands and the waves grow still and
　　calm.[10]

40 A woman has furtively touched the hem of your sacred garment
And at once she is healed: the pallor leaves her face
And the haemorrhage which had flowed unceasingly stops.[11]
He saw a young man snatched away with the passing of sweet
youth
And his bereaved mother escorting him to his grave with
farewell tears.
'Arise,' he said. The young man gets up and is given back to his
mother.[12]
Already for four days Lazarus had been deprived of sunlight,
buried in the tomb,
But Christ restores his breath and commands him to live:
The breath restored once more enters into the decaying flesh.[13]
He walks across the sea's surface, he treads the top of the waves;
50 The shifting waters of the deep offer a suspended path
And the waves do not open under the weight of his sacred
steps.[14]
One that for long had roared in chains, within a cavernous
tomb,
Out of his mind and driven by wild frenzy, leaps forth
And rushes out to beg for help when he knows Christ is
there.[15]
The disease with the thousand slippery devils is driven out,
And seizes hold of an unclean herd of filthy pigs,
But the frenzied animals plunge deep into the black waters.[16]
Bring in the leftovers from the feast in twelve baskets;
Thousands of guests are now amply filled
60 By eating the five loaves of bread and the two fishes.[17]
You are our nourishment, our bread, you the tastiness that lasts
for ever.
Anyone who partakes of your meal will never be hungry again,
Not filling his empty belly, but refreshing his life-giving forces.
The ears' blocked passage, incapable of hearing sounds,
Is cleared of all its thick obstructions on Christ's orders,
So that it can enjoy voices, now that whispers can pass through.
Every illness yields before him, every weakness is driven off,
The tongue speaks out though bound for long in silence,
And the sick man joyfully carries his bed through the city.
70 Indeed, in his goodness he even enters Hell itself so that
salvation
Should not be denied those down there. The gates are broken
down and give way,

The bolts are ripped off and the hinges fall to pieces.
The gate, ready to receive those rushing in but unyielding for
    those going back
Is unbarred and yields up the dead, now that the law is
    overturned
And the dark doorway stands open for the dead to pass through
    once more.
But while God illuminated the caves of death with golden
    light,
When he brought bright daylight to the astonished darkness,
The sad stars grew pale in the gloomy sky.
In its grief the sun fled, clad in the dark clothes of mourning,
80  And left the fiery heavens, withdrawing in sorrow.
The world is said to have shuddered in fear at the chaos of
    eternal night.
Speak, my sonorous heart, speak with nimble tongue,
Tell of the victory of the passion, tell of the triumphant cross,[18]
Sing of the banner which shines forth as a sign upon our
    foreheads.
How strange the miracle of the wound inflicted in his
    astounding death.
Here there flowed a stream of blood, there a stream of water;
Water of course provides a bath, while a prize is won with
    blood.
The serpent saw the sacred body sacrificed,
Saw and at once he lost the venom of his inflamed gall,
90  Wounded as he was by a great pain, his hissing throat
    shattered.
What did it profit you, wicked serpent, when the world was
    new
To have destroyed the first creature by means of your cunning
    persuasion?
The mortal form has washed away its sin by receiving God.
He who brings salvation gave himself up to a brief experience
    of death
So that he might teach the dead, buried long since, to return
When the bonds of their former sins had been torn apart.
Then the fathers and many holy people, following their creator
As he leads the way when he returns on the third day,
Put on garments of flesh and come forth from their tombs.
100 You would see the limbs re-assembling from dry ashes
And the cold dust grow warm as it takes on flesh again

And bones, sinews and entrails covered with skin to bind them.
Afterwards when he had destroyed death and restored man,
He ascended victorious to the lofty judgement seat of the
    Father on high,
Bringing back to heaven the outstanding glory of his passion.
Glory to you, judge of the dead, glory to you, king of the
    living,
You who on the right hand of your father's throne are famed for
    your virtues,
You will come thence as a just avenger of all sins.
Let old people praise you, and the young; let the band of little
    children,
110 Let the company of mothers and virgins and innocent little
    girls
Praise you with voices in harmony and with modest songs.
Let the gliding waters of the rivers, the banks of the shores,
The rain, heat, snow, frost, woodland and breezes, night and
    day,
Join together in praising you throughout all ages.


## Psychomachia 454–632

*Avarice's success in battle; Avarice's speech; Avarice and Generosity clash; Generosity's speech to the troops*

It is said that Avarice, whose dress had a large pocket in front,
Snatched with her hooked hand everything valuable
Left behind by voracious Indulgence; with mouth wide open
She looked covetously at the pretty trifles as she collected bits
    of gold
Lying among the heaps of sand; but not content to fill her
    pocket
She took delight in stuffing the filthy lucre into bags
460 And making purses swell, heavy with stolen goods
Which she covered with her left hand to conceal them, hiding
    them
Under her cloak; for her right hand quickly snatches up her loot,
Using her nails as hard as bronze to pick up the spoils.
Worry, Hunger, Fear, Anxiety, Perjury, Pallor,
Corruption, Trickery, Lies, Insomnia and Meanness,
All the different Furies push forward, accompanying this
    monster.

Meanwhile, like rabid wolves, Crimes are also on the attack
Rushing around all over the battlefield,
The offspring of Avarice, fed by her black milk.
470 If a soldier sees the helmet of his brother and fellow-soldier
Flashing with sparkling gems, he does not fear to draw
His sword and strike the skull with the blade, although he is a
        comrade,
So that he can rip the jewels from his brother's head.
If a son happens to catch sight of his father's corpse
Which has met its death in war, he eagerly pulls off the belt
With its shining studs, together with the bloodstained armour.
Civil war collects booty from its own relations
And the insatiable desire for possessions spares not
Its own family; unnatural greed robs its own children.
480 Such was the carnage produced among the people
By Avarice, the conqueror of the world: wounding them in
        different ways
She destroyed them in their thousands; one she blinded,
Gouging out his eyes and allowing him to wander sightless
As if in the darkness of night and to stumble over many
        obstacles
Without letting him use a stick to feel the dangers in his path.
Another she captures by means of his sight and tricks him as he
        looks:
She shows him something splendid and as he tries to reach it
He is unexpectedly hit by a weapon; wounded deep within his
        heart
He groans, feeling the metal driven into him.
490 Many she drives headlong into open fires,
Not permitting them to avoid the flames where melts the gold
The greedy speculator is after, he who will burn with it.
Avarice seizes every type of person, every mortal being
She attacks and destroys: there is no vice more destructive
In all the world. It overwhelms the lives of people of this world
With such terrible disasters, condemning them to hell.
In fact, if it is to be believed, she even dared to attack
The priests of the Lord who happened to be the leaders
Standing in front of the lines, fighting to defend the virtues
500 And blowing loudly on their trumpets.
Perhaps she would have dipped her weapon in innocent blood
If valiant Reason, the only loyal companion of Levi's race,
Had not thrust her shield forward to parry the blow, protecting

Her noble foster-children from her grim enemy's attack.
They remain safe with Reason's help, they remain immune
From all the tumult, undaunted; the spear of Avarice
Wounds a few of them just slightly, hardly grazing
The surface of their skin. This wicked pest was stunned to see
Her weapons pushed away from the virtuous heroes' throats.

510 She groans, and raging with anger speaks these furious words:
'Alas, we are beaten, paralysed, and our power cannot produce
Its usual force; spent is our fierce passion to cause harm
Which used to break through the hearts of men everywhere
With unbeaten force; for no man has by nature
Ever been so hard-hearted that he would be tough enough
To scorn money or remain unaffected by our gold.
We have destroyed every kind of person: the tender, harsh and
    stern,
The educated as well as the uneducated, the stupid and the
    wise,
Even the pure have fallen victim to my hand with the impure.

520 Thus I alone have seized all those hidden by the river Styx
With its greedy eddies. It is to us that rich Tartarus owes
All the people it contains: what the generations bring forth
    belongs to us;
The world's confusion, its frenzied activity, belongs to us.
How is it that our robust strength has lost its power and glory
And fortune mocks our arms which have grown useless?
The golden image of glittering money is despised
By Christians, despised are silver coins and all treasure
Is despicable in their eyes, for its brightness has grown dim.
What means this disdain in which they are trained? Did we not
    triumph

530 Over Iscariot, one of the foremost disciples who shared God's
    table?
Though bound by the obligations of a guest he deceived Jesus
Who was well aware; as Judas put his hand to the dish at the
    same time,
He was hit by our weapon as a result of burning greed
For he had bought the infamous field with the price of God's
    blood,
God who was his friend; but he would pay for these acres with a
    strangled neck.
Jericho, too, at the time of its destruction, had seen
The power of my hand, when Achan the victor fell.[19]

Famed for the slaughter he caused, proud of having destroyed
    the walls,
He succumbed to the gold captured from the vanquished
    enemy,
540 Picking up from the forbidden ashes an attractive but accursed
    thing,
In his insatiable desire for the grim spoils lying among the
    ruins.
It did him no good to be of a noble tribe or to derive his
    ancestry
From Judah who would one day be famed as a relative of Christ,
A patriarch fortunate to have such a descendant.
Let those who would like a family like Achan's also like a death
    like his!
Let those who are of the same race share the same punishment.
Why do I hesitate to deceive by some trick the people of
    Judah
Or the people of the high priest ( for that is what Aaron was
    said to be),
Since I am not on a par with them on the field of battle?
550 It matters not whether victory is won by weapons or deceit.'
Her speech was finished: abandoning her fierce look and
    terrifying weapons
She transformed herself into a respectable-looking creature.
With her austere countenance and clothing she resembled a
    virtue,
The one men call Thrift, who likes to live frugally
And to save what she has, never grasping anything in greed.
With her apparent carefulness she won praise for the behaviour
    she feigned.
The deceitful Bellona puts on this disguise
So as to be thought a thrifty virtue rather than a greedy pest.
She also covers her snaky tresses with a thin covering
560 Of motherly love so that the white veil might hide
The fury lurking beneath and with brutal rage concealed
She can use a pleasant term – 'care for one's children' – to refer
To what is really snatching, stealing, greedily hiding what one
    has taken.
By means of such illusions she mocks people, deceiving them,
And gullible as they are they follow the deadly monster,
Believing this to be the work of virtue; then the wicked Fury
    traps them

For they readily go along with her and she holds them in tight
     handcuffs.
The leaders are shocked, the troops thrown into confusion,
The battle lines of the virtues waver, led astray
570 By the monster's double guise, not knowing what to trust –
Is she friend or foe? This changing and ambiguous deadly
     monster
With her doubtful appearance makes them uncertain of what
     they see,
When suddenly Generosity, gnashing her teeth, rushes forward
Into the midst of the battle, engaging in the fight to help her
     allies.
She had been placed at the back of the army but was destined
To put an end to the battle, making sure nothing bad remained.
She had thrown from her shoulders all that she carried, she
     marched on
Stripped of all clothing, having relieved herself of many bags.
For she had been burdened by riches and the weight of money
580 But she was unencumbered now, having shown pity to the poor,
Caring for them with kindness and generosity, sharing her
     family wealth.
Rich in faith now, she looked at her empty wallet,
Counting up the sum from the return of interest which would
     last for ever.
At the sight of this invincible Virtue's destructive power
Avarice stood still, paralysed with shock, out of her mind,
Convinced that she would die: for what deception remained to
     overcome someone
Who had trampled on the world? How could she use worldly
     temptations
To destroy her and make her grasp again the gold she had rejected?
As she stands there trembling the brave Virtue seizes her in a
     tight grip,
590 Strangling her neck, squeezing her throat dry and bloodless
And crushing it; her arms are shackles tightened round the
     throat
Beneath the chin and from the narrow windpipe
They squeeze out the life: it is convulsed and snatched away,
Not by a wound but by the obstruction of the air passage:
Life suffers death, shut up within the prison of the veins.
As Avarice struggles, Generosity presses down on her with
     knees and feet,

Pierces her ribs and tears open her panting sides.
Then she rips the spoils from the corpse: the foul bits
Of crude gold and the metal not yet purified in the furnace,
600 And the money bags eaten away by large numbers of worms,
As well as tarnished coins covered in rust, all these things,
Long hoarded, the victorious Virtue distributes and hands out
    to the needy,
Presenting gifts to the poor from what she has confiscated.
Then she looks round at the crowds surrounding her
And with a look of jubilation she shouts out cheerfully amidst
    the thousands:
'Give up your military enterprise, good people, and leave your
    weapons!
The cause of such a great evil lies dead; now that the voracious
    greed
For gain is destroyed, the good may have some peace.
Perfect peace is to wish for nothing more than what normal use
    demands,
610 For simple food to restore our feeble limbs
And a single garment to cover them, without excess,
And not to be led beyond the limits of nature's satisfaction.
As you set off on your journey, take no rucksack with you,
Do not worry about carrying a change of clothing.
Do not fear what tomorrow may bring or that your stomach[20]
Might have nothing to eat: each new day brings the necessary
    food.
Surely you see how birds do not plan for the next day?
    Confident
That God will provide them with food, they have no worries.
Birds of little value are certain they will not lack food,
620 And the sparrows that one buys so cheaply have an unfailing
    trust
That the all-powerful Lord will ensure they do not perish,
While you, the object of God's care and the image of Christ,
Do you worry that your creator might one day abandon you?
Do not fear, my men! He who gives life also gives food.
Seek in divine teaching the sustenance that brings light:
It nourishes by increasing the hope of an incorruptible life;
Forget your body, for he who created it does not forget
To provide food and to supply your limbs with what they need.'
With these words she dispelled their cares: Fear, Hardship and
    Violence

630 Together with Crime and Deception that denies the promise
    given,
Were driven off and fled. Now that the enemy had been put to
    flight
Kindly Peace put a stop to war; every terror was disarmed.

## Peristephanon 3

*Hymn in honour of the passion of the blessed martyr Eulalia*

Eulalia, the holy virgin, noble in her birth,
Even nobler in the manner of her death,
Adorns with her bones and honours with her love
Her beloved Merida which in its richness
Brought her forth.

In the extreme west lies this place
Which produced this outstanding ornament:
The city makes it powerful, its people make it rich
But the blood of martyrdom and the virgin's tomb
10 Increase its power.

She had reached the age of twelve
And passed through twelve winters
When her grim austerity on the crackling pyre
Made the executioners tremble with fear
For she considered torture pleasant.

Already earlier she had given an indication
That she was striving towards the Father's throne
And that her body was not destined for marriage,
When as a little girl she rejected toys
20 And did not know how to play;

She showed no interest in amber beads, cried at roses
And disapproved of golden necklaces.
While still very young she had an austere look
And a modest deportment,
Behaving like a grey-haired old man.

But when the raging pest
Attacked the servants of the Lord,

And cruelly ordered the Christians
To burn incense and offer animals' entrails
30    To the death-dealing gods,

Eulalia's saintly spirit raged:
In her fierceness she was prepared
To triumph in the violent battle;
Her young breast panted only for God,
A woman provoking the weapons of men.

But her mother in her loving care arranged
For the spirited virgin to be concealed at home
In a remote rural area, far from the city,
To prevent the wild girl, in her desire for death,
40    From rushing to pay the price of martyrdom.

But Eulalia hated to endure idleness
In a delay she considered shameful:
At night she pushed the door when no one was looking,
Opening it to escape from her imprisonment,
Then hurried away along minor paths.

She hastened along over wasteland
Covered with brambles, her feet lacerated,
But accompanied by a band of angels;
Although the night's silence terrified her,
50    Yet she had their light to guide her.

Just as the troop of our noble ancestors
Had a pillar of light,[21] whose bright torch
Could cut through the darkness
And provide a path through the night,
Causing the darkness to be dispelled,

In the same way the pious virgin following the path
Through the night was rewarded with daylight
And was not enveloped by the darkness
As she fled from the kingdom of Egypt,
60    Preparing to pass beyond the stars.

She made swift progress by staying awake all night
And travelled many miles before

The eastern shores opened up the heavens;
In the morning she proudly approached the tribunal
And took her stand amid the symbols of power.

She shouts out, 'Tell me, what is this madness
That drives your souls headlong to destruction,
Making your self-destructive hearts
Abase themselves before idols of polished stone
70   And deny God who is Father of all?

You wretched people, are you seeking
The race of Christians? Here I am,
An enemy of the demonic rites,
I crush the idols beneath my feet
And confess God with heart and lips.

Isis, Apollo and Venus are nothing,
Maximian[22] himself is nothing:
Being human artefacts, they are nothing;
Worshipping human artefacts, he is nothing;
80   Both are worthless and both are nothing.

Maximian is the master of the world
And yet himself a slave to stones;
Let him prostitute and vow his own head
To his own powers;
Why must he batter noble hearts?

A good leader and outstanding judge
Feeds on innocent blood
And greedy for their pious bodies
He tears apart their temperate flesh,
90   Delights in torturing their faith.

So come on, torturer, burn and cut,
Tear apart the limbs formed from clay!
It is easy to break something fragile
But torment's pain cannot pierce
The soul deep within.'

Aroused to fury by her words
The praetor said, 'Take her away at once,

Lictor, and pile on the tortures!
Let her realize that our nation's gods exist
100 And the emperor's power is great.

But I would like you, before you die,
If possible to retract your wickedness,
You fierce little girl. Consider
The joys you are sacrificing,
Which an honourable marriage would bring.

Your shattered family accompanies you
With their tears and your noble relatives
In their distress bewail the fact
That you are being put to death so young
110 When you were on the point of marriage.

Are you not moved by the wedding's golden splendour
Or the tender affection of the old people
Who are disheartened by your impulsive behaviour?
Look at the instruments ready to inflict
An excruciating death:

Either your head will be cut off with a sword
Or wild beasts will tear your limbs apart
Or you will be put among the smoking flames
And your family will scream and cry for you
120 As you dissolve into ashes.

What, I ask, is the difficulty in avoiding this?
If you were willing, little girl, just to touch
A little salt, a pinch of incense
With your fingertips, this terrible punishment
Would be averted.'

To this the martyr made no reply but raged
And spat into the tyrant's eyes;
Then she smashed the statues
And ground beneath her feet the grain
130 Placed on the incense burners.

Then without delay the two executioners
Slashed her tender breast

And struck the young girl on both sides
With the claw,[23] cutting her to the bone
While Eulalia counted the marks.

'Look, O Lord, how you are inscribed upon me!
What pleasure I get from reading these letters
Which are a mark of your victory, O Christ!
Even the purple colour of the blood they cause to flow
140 Speaks your sacred name.'

Without tears or sighs she spoke these words.
Full of joy she feels no fear
And experiences no dread or pain
As her limbs are coloured by the fresh blood
And her skin washed by this warm stream.

Then came the final torture:
Not a wounding and tearing
To the bone and no lacerated skin
But all around the torch's flames
150 Blazed against her sides and front.

She let her fragrant hair flow down
Over her breast, floating over her shoulders
So as to conceal her modesty
And her girlish beauty with the covering
Of her head exposed.

But the crackling flames raced up to her face,
Taking hold of her head as they spread
Through her hair and reached the top in triumph.
The girl, longing for a quick death,
160 Welcomes the fire and laps it up.

Then suddenly a dove flies forth,
Whiter than snow, and is seen to leave
The martyr's mouth, making for the stars;
This was Eulalia's spirit, milk-white,
Innocent and swift.

As her soul departs, her neck goes slack
And the fiery pyre dies down;

Peace is granted to her lifeless limbs;
In the sky her spirit celebrates in triumph,
170 Quickly reaching the temples on high.

The judge himself saw the bird
Fly from the girl's mouth in front of them all;
Utterly stunned and thunderstruck
He leapt up, fleeing from what he had done,
And in terror, too, the lictor fled.

Look how the icy winter brings the snow,
Covering the whole forum,
And as Eulalia's body lies there
Beneath the freezing sky, snow covers it
180 As if with a linen burial cloth.

No need for the loving tears of men
Whose custom it is to celebrate the last rites;
No need, either, for the ceremony provoking tears;
The very elements, at God's command,
Perform your funerary rites, little girl.

Now Merida is the site of your tomb,
Vettonia's illustrious colony,
Past which flows the famous river Ana:
Rushing along with its swirling green waters
190 It washes your lovely walls.

Here the bright marble, both imported
And local, shines brightly,
Illuminating the dignified halls,
While in its bosom the venerable earth
Preserves your remains and sacred ashes.

The bright roofs flash forth above
With their golden ceilings
And the floor is adorned with mosaics,
So you might think it was a meadow
200 Coloured by many kinds of flowers.

Go gather the purple violets,
Cut down the blood red saffron.

The merry wintertime is not devoid of these
For the ice melts, no longer holding fields in its grip,
Allowing you to pile baskets full of flowers.

Boys and girls, distribute these gifts
Made from the luxuriant foliage.
But I will bring garlands to the procession
Woven from dactylic verses,
210 Of little value, fading, yet festive.

In this way we delight to do homage
To the bones and the altar above them,
While she is seated at the feet of God
And looks down on this, protecting
Her people, propitiated by this song.

# CYPRIAN THE POET

## Introduction

The set of poems amounting to 5,250 lines that are now attributed to Cyprian of Gaul (or Cyprian the Poet) had for long circulated under various names[1] and in various forms but it is now thought that the author of this work is likely to have lived in southern Gaul in the early fifth century and may indeed have been the Cyprian to whom Jerome addressed his *Letter* 140. The work, which takes the form of a paraphrase of the historical books of the Old Testament, may be unfinished for we have only verse paraphrases of the seven books from Genesis to Judges (together with a few fragments from Kings and Chronicles), for which reason it is often referred to as the *Heptateuch*.

The fact that the paraphrase keeps closely to the *Itala* (pre-Vulgate) text of the Bible has led some critics to suggest that Juvencus was the author, offering an Old Testament paraphrase to set beside his New Testament one. In fact, not only does the poet keep closely to the text and concentrate on the narrative sections but he actually omits entire sections, particularly from the text of Numbers and Leviticus. He does, however, expand on occasion, as in the account of the crossing of the Red Sea in Exodus and in the story of Joseph from Genesis. Furthermore, he reorganizes the scriptural chronology to a certain extent,[2] for example combining the Tree of Life and the Tree of Knowledge, and postponing the command to multiply and the prohibition of the fruit of the tree until after Eve's creation. On the whole, he emphasizes God's benevolence to mankind, as when he shows God making clothes for Adam and Eve when they become aware of their nakedness. He also plays down the after-effects of the Fall which he describes in terms of a visit by the serpent at night promising the return of daylight if Adam and Eve eat of the fruit: the humans, understandably seduced by this promise, are deceived into acting in disobedience to God. The *Heptateuch* may be less overtly didactic or allegorical than other biblical epics but it does contain some interesting interpretative details, as Nodes has shown,[3] and occasionally the poet does attempt to bring out the soteriological implications of the Old Testament account, as when he interprets the three young men who visit Abraham (Genesis 18) as types of the Trinity (Genesis line 611).

The poems are in hexameters, apart from three lyrical passages (the song of Moses at the crossing of the Red Sea, the people at the well of Beer, and the song of Moses before his death) written in hendecasyllables. The poet introduces a number of neologisms but on the whole his language is modelled on that of Virgil and Lucretius in particular (from whom he sometimes cites entire verses), but also shows traces of Catullus, Horace, Ovid, Persius, Juvenal, Juvencus, Paulinus and Prudentius. It does not appear that the *Heptateuch* was widely read in the following centuries, though there are references to the work in a number of early English writers, such as Aldhelm, Bede, Alcuin and Aethelwulf.

The passage translated below tells of the creation of Adam and Eve, the serpent's seduction, and God's punishment. Cyprian rearranges the biblical narrative of the first three chapters of Genesis as shown in the notes.

## Text

Latin text: CSEL 23 (1891).

Example of Latin verse form; hexameters

*Genesis* 1–6

Principio dominus caelum terramque locavit:
Namque erat informis fluctuque abscondita tellus
Immensusque deus super aequora vasta meabat,
Dum chaos et nigrae fuscabant cuncta tenebrae;
Hos dum disiungi iussit, a cardine fatur:
'Lux fiat!' et clare nituerunt omnia mundo.

## Genesis 25–133

When the divine power had established these things by his command,[4]

He noticed that there was no one to manage affairs on earth
And so he said, 'Let us make man exactly similar to us in
    appearance
And then he can have dominion over the whole world.'
And although he could create man by his Word alone,
30  Yet he was kind enough to lead him with his holy hand
And breathed from his divine lungs into the insensible
    creature's chest.[5]
When he saw that man was formed as it were in his own image,
He judged that he should not remain alone to worry over
    nagging cares.[6]
And so he at once poured sleep over the creature's eyes[7]
So that he could gently remove a rib out of which to form
    woman,
So the combined substance might strengthen the double limbs.
She was given the name of Eve, signifying 'life':[8]
Because of her, it is usual for children to leave their parents
And to cleave to their spouses, abandoning their homes.
40  Having finished his creation, God rested on the seventh day,
Establishing it as a holy day for the enjoyment of future ages.[9]
At once, when all the living beings had been paraded in order,
Adam who had been granted practical understanding and
    ingenuity
Gave to them all individually a name intended to last.[10]
God then graciously addressed him, together with Eve, his
    wife:
'Increase in numbers by having children throughout future ages
So that the sky and earth may be filled with your offspring
And as my heirs, you may pick the various fruits
Which the woods and fields produce from their rich soil.'[11]
50  After this speech he established paradise in that beautiful
    place[12]
And he looked upon the light of the first sun.
Among the plants there grew a tree with deadly fruit
Producing a taste of life and death combined.
At the centre of this place there flows a river with a pure
    stream[13]
Irrigating the lovely gardens with its clear waters,
And cutting a fourfold channel with its rippling stream.
The rich Phisonus flows with gold-bearing waters
And with its noisy gurgling it polishes bright gems –
One gem is called the prasine, another the carbuncle –

60 As its clear waters lap the land of Havilah.
The second is Geon, enriching the Ethiopians as it flows,
While the third is the Tigris, connected to the lovely
    Euphrates,
Whose fast-flowing stream drives a distinct furrow through
    Assyria.
Here Adam was placed as guardian, together with his loyal
    wife;[14]
And he became a farmer because of these words from the
    Thunderer:
'Do not be afraid to pick those fruits that are lawful,
Created by the flourishing woods on their leafy branches;
But beware lest by chance you pick an apple that is harmful,
Produced from the double sap for different purposes.'
70 Meanwhile the deep darkness of night held them fast in their
    blindness
And no garments clothed their bodies, newly created as they
    were.
Through this place, this garden with its ripe fruits,[15]
A foaming snake, outdoing all the other animals in cunning,
Was slithering silently with chilly coils;
Devising lies inspired by envy in its embittered mind,
It made an assault on the woman, testing her susceptibility.
'Tell me, why are you afraid of the apple tree's wholesome fruit?
Has God not blessed all the fruits that are produced?
In fact if you choose to pick the honey-sweet food,
80 The golden world will smile from its starry heights.'
She refused, fearing to touch the forbidden branches,
But her weakness of mind overcame her resolve.
As soon as she bit into the ripe fruit with her snow-white teeth,
The clear sky, unblemished by a single cloud, shone bright.
Then when the seductively sweet taste entered her mouth,
It impelled her to offer it as a gift to her unsuspecting husband.
As soon as he tasted it, darkness was wiped away and his
    shining eyes
Flashed forth, while the world shone bright around him.
And when they both noticed that their bodies were naked,
90 They covered with fig leaves the parts they saw as shameful.
It happened that as the light of the sun was setting,
They heard the sound of the Lord: in fear they looked for a
    place to hide.
Then the Lord of heaven rebuked Adam in his shame:

'Tell me, where are you now?' Adam replied humbly with these
  words:
'Great Lord, I tremble in my fearful heart when you address me,
And in my nakedness I am suffering from cold and fear.'
Then the Lord said, 'Who was it who gave you the deadly
  fruit?'
'This woman gave it to me, claiming that her eyes had been
Suddenly suffused with a bright light and that the clear sky
100 And sun and stars of heaven had shone forth for her.'
At once God's anger struck terror into Eve who was distraught
When the Almighty asked who was responsible for the
  forbidden deed.
Then she explained, 'I fell for the serpent's persuasive words –
It deceived me with its lies and seductive request.
For lacing its words with a viper's poison,
It told me that these apples were sweeter than all the rest.'
At once the Almighty cursed the serpent for what it had done
And commanded that the monster should live hated by all,
Gliding along on its extended belly, and the soil should be its
  food.
110 There would be antagonism for all time to come
Between human sensation and the slithering snake:
With its head on a level with its belly it would crawl
In pursuit of people's legs and heels, sliding up close behind
  them.
The woman pitiably tricked by its treacherous persuasion
Is ordered to accept that childbirth will be risky and painful,
And devotedly to endure subjection to her husband.
'But you, who thought your wife's opinion was reliable,
She who had yielded to the cruel serpent,
You will suffer the affliction of hard work all your life.
120 For instead of the shoots of the wheat harvest,
Thistles will spring up and thorn-bushes with their sharp
  prickles,
So that physically exhausted and mentally dejected,
You will often groan as you produce your food, a cause of
  anxiety,
Until in the evening of your life, when death is at hand,
You will give your body back to the level earth whence it
  came.'
Then the Lord filled them, terrified as they were, with a
  weariness of life

And removed them, dispirited, from the blessed garden placing
    them opposite it;
He turned them out of the gates, putting a fire to block their
    path.
In the swift heat the cherubim are revealed
130 While the fiery sword blazes down, rolling forth flames.
The Lord then sewed together skins stripped from animal flesh
So that their limbs would not freeze in the numbing cold,
And with warm clothes he wrapped their naked bodies.

# SEDULIUS

## Introduction

Little is known about the life of Caelius Sedulius, the author not only of the *Carmen Paschale* (*Easter Song*), but of a prose version of this poem entitled the *Opus Paschale*, as well as two hymns, one a brief history of salvation in fifty-five couplets (*Cantemus socii*), the other the very famous abecedarian hymn, comprising twenty-three stanzas of iambic dimeters and giving a summary of Christ's life from birth to resurrection (*A solis ortus cardine*). Sedulius' work is quoted by poets and writers of the second half of the fifth century and it would seem that he himself was writing in Italy around the year 430.

The *Carmen Paschale*, from which three excerpts are translated below, derived its name from St Paul's statement at 1 Corinthians 5:7: 'For Christ our paschal lamb has been sacrificed'. The poem is 'paschal' because it deals with Christ's sacrifice for our sake. It is the Passion and Resurrection of Christ that form the climax of the work for these events are central to the Christian faith. In his dedicatory letter addressed to a certain Macedonius, Sedulius tells the familiar story of how, after years in a secular career, the poet has turned to God and wishes now to use his talents in the service of the truth. He has decided to write poetry because, as he admits, people find poetry more attractive and it will therefore be more effective for his purpose which is to lead others to the truth. If the pagans use poetic art to tell things which are fictitious, why should Sedulius not follow David in using poetry for a more important and truthful subject?

The work may originally have consisted of four books but it now exists in five. The first tells of miracles from the Old Testament in order to demonstrate Christ's power, for in his eagerness to defend an orthodox view of Christ against Arian doctrines,[1] Sedulius is determined at every possible opportunity to point out that Christ is both fully human and fully divine, often using paradox to emphasize this fact, as when he says that Christ was both asleep and awake during the storm (Matthew 8:24). The second book recounts the infancy and baptism of Christ, his choice of Apostles and gives a commentary on the Lord's prayer; the third and fourth books concentrate on Jesus' miracles, mostly based on the account given in the Gospel according to St Matthew. The final book tells of events in the period between the Last Supper and Christ's ascension.

Sedulius' poem, like that of Juvencus, is clearly influenced by Virgil's *Aeneid* but the *Carmen Paschale* is not merely a versification of the Bible narrative in Virgilian hexameters. Sedulius is selective in the events he recounts and it is clear that he has an ambitious purpose in writing. He is more concerned with Christ's deeds than his words, for his interest lies in the soteriological implications of the Incarnation, rather than in moral advice. He wishes to provide a summary of salvation history, tying the events of the Old Testament in with those of the New to show how God's purpose has been working through Christ throughout the course of history. He uses typology to connect the Old and the New Testaments, as when he points out that Mary has reversed the evil brought into the world by Eve, and he uses allegory to bring out the spiritual significance of the events of Christ's life on earth. His style is vivid and lively, with the literal account alternating with passages of interpretation, and with frequent expressions of the poet's outrage or wonder.

The *Carmen Paschale* well deserved the popularity it rapidly achieved and maintained throughout the Middle Ages, becoming one of the most widely read of Latin poems, as is clear from the number of manuscripts in which this poem occurs and the frequency with which it is referred to. His reworking of the account into prose form, producing the so-called *opus geminatum*, influenced the production of similar double compositions by Aldhelm, Bede and Alcuin.

## Texts

Latin text: PL 19, CSEL 10 (1885).

Example of Latin verse form; hexameters

*Carmen Paschale* 1.23–6

Cur ego Daviticis adsuetus cantibus odas
Chordarum resonare decem sanctoque verenter

Stare choro et placidis caelestia psallere verbis,
Clara salutiferi taceam miracula Christi?

## Carmen Paschale 1.136–159

*Based on Exodus 14:21–22; 16:13–21 and 17:1–6*

The dark waters of the sea parted and opened, offering a way
    through
As they rolled back on either side; the earth was exposed,
Stripped of its familiar waters and on foot the mass of people
Entered the sea, though the sea was gone, and the dry waters
140 Were stunned to see strange feet walking through the deep.
Nature changed its course and the people went right in
Through the middle of the sea, already undergoing a primitive
    baptism,
For Christ was their leader, as the reading clearly proclaims:
*The voice of the Lord is over many waters,*[2] and the voice is the
    Word.
Christ the Word is present; he who governs the two Testaments
Of the Law existing in harmony, opened up the ancient abyss,
So that the teaching that followed might walk on dry and level
    land.
Why should I mention how the innumerable hordes
Ate of angelic foods with bread from heaven and how the
    people
150 Fed on the airborne sweetness of divine nectar from the clouds,
Obtaining their meals from the rain and their food from the
    showers.
Then when the mass of people were thirsting in the wilderness
Where the ground was too dry and where the land had long
    lain sick
Because of the lack of water and they had lost all hope
Of drink and life, they were suddenly able to draw water
From the barren rock: a stream flowed from the sterile rock
And the parched stone poured forth a new drink.
And so in these three things were granted sacred gifts:
Christ was the bread, Christ the rock, Christ in the waters.

## 5.20–68 (The Last Supper)

*Based on Matthew 26:17–25 and 47–49*

20  Then he celebrated the traditional passover festival
By means of the sacred duties of the annual meal; he humbled
    himself
Though he was the master, and leaving his disciples a dear
    example
He got up and gladly served his servants; equipped
With a linen cloth he paid them every honour,
So much so that while voluntarily washing the feet of all the
    disciples
He did not even exclude Judas, although he knew he was
    planning
A wicked betrayal. But that honour, cruel traitor,
Did not allow you to remain with clean feet,
For you were polluted by your thoughts, like every tomb
30  On the outside covered with a coating of whitewash
While the inside is filled with filth and rotting corpses.[3]
The Lord was well aware of his treachery and exposed
The one planning the future crime by handing him the bread –
He who was himself the bread that would be handed over. For
    then
The Lord blessed the two gifts of his own body and blood
As he distributed the food and drink which signifies that never,
For eternity, will faithful and pure souls experience thirst and
    hunger.
At once a most foul spirit entered into Judas
Where envy dwelled, and taking up its weapons
40  It caused a war to start of servant against master,
Determined on a dreadful crime at any price. He is not to
    blame
For the reward; it is to the deed that blame attaches.
Blinded by the reward of a small amount of silver
He accepted thirty coins, thereby acting as criminally
As if he were to capture all the kingdoms of the earth,
And the riches of the sea and the whole sky with its scudding
    clouds;
For all the good things of this world would not suffice
To pay for the shedding of the blood of Christ, the mighty one,
The father of the world, to whom Judas also owes his birth.

50 If only he had been doomed within a barren womb, unable
 To experience the day of his birth and had never
 Breathed in this life's gentle breezes with their vital breath,
 But been buried in unconsciousness for ever; it would have been
   better
 For the wretch never to have known this life than lose it once
   given.
 Or once born, unluckily, he should have been deprived at once
 Of the gift of light, just like the dust which a strong wind
 Flings forth from the face of the earth; in rapid whirling
   movements
 It is scattered into the empty darkness, less visible than clouds
   of mist.
 You murderous, savage, reckless and rebellious fool,
60 Treacherous, cruel, deceitful, corrupt and unjust,
 Merciless traitor, ruthless betrayer, wicked criminal,
 Do you lead the way as you escort the grim men with their
   swords?
 When you start to march with the wicked soldiers, menacing
 With their swords and sticks, you press your mouth to his,
 Mixing poison with honey, betraying the Lord by a show of
   affection.
 Why pretend to be his friend, greeting him with amicable
   deceit?
 Never does peace conspire against terrifying swords
 Or the wolf offer kisses of aggression to the gentle lamb.


## 5.164–244 (The Crucifixion)

*These verses are based on the account given in Matthew 27:27–51, supple-
mented by the details from Luke 23:39–43 telling of the crucified robbers'
different reactions to Christ.*

 When the holy one went out after being handed over for
   punishment
 To the ruthless soldiers, they clothed him in a cheap robe
 Coloured with scarlet dye, so that his whole blood-red
   appearance
 Would be an image of death; his magnificent head was
   encircled
 With a crown woven of thorns, because in his mercy
 He took upon himself all the thorns of our misfortunes.

170 In his hand they placed a reed signifying that the sovereignty of
   this world
Is shifting, ineffectual, uncertain, empty, impotent.
Then he took off the borrowed clothes and put on his own,
Doubtless because he was going to lay aside the covering of
   human flesh,
Changing himself in the same way so as to carry nothing
   mutable
175 When after death he rose again, clothed in his own majesty.[4]
177 It is clear that it was not without divine authority
That he was given wine mixed with gall; he took it
But when the sharp taste touched his lips he pushed it from his
   mouth
180 For he who was shortly to have a taste of bitter death
Was preparing to scorn it by returning in the flesh.[5]
Then at once he was hung high on the spreading cross,
Transforming the anger of the crisis by means of loving
   devotion.
He himself was the peace of the cross and illuminating the
   violent
Forces with his own limbs he clothed the punishment with
   honour,
Giving a sign that it was not a punishment but salvation,
And sanctifying the tortures he suffered, he blessed them.
Everyone should know that the shape of the cross is to be
   revered
For it bore our Lord in his triumph and by a powerful logic
190 It brings together the four corners of the world.
The radiant East shines forth from the creator's head,
His holy feet are licked by the sun setting in the West,
His right hand holds the North, his left supports the centre of
   the sky;
The whole of Nature lives from the creator's limbs
And Christ rules throughout the world, encompassed by the cross.
On it a heading also was inscribed: 'This is the King of the Jews',
So that nothing would lack divinity; for heaven arranged
That this was recorded in Hebrew, in Latin and in Greek.
Thus the one faith teaches us to call on the one King three
   times.[6]
200 Lots were thrown for the clothes they stripped from him
So the sacred robe remaining whole might warn against schism
   from Christ.[7]

And furthermore on either side of the innocent Christ they
    place
Two criminals, though their identical sentence does not mean
That all three deserved the same; for indeed
When the holy one hung between the villainous robbers,
The punishment of the three was the same but the guilt of two
    was not.
For these are guilty to the world on account of many crimes,
While for this one the world is guilty, redeemed by his just
    blood.
Yet the ruler of all things, even in the midst of his suffering,
210 Did not lose the authority of his power. For the just judge,
Looking at both men, chose one and condemned the other,
Weighing what each deserved in his lofty balance.
For one, who even in death continued to live aggressively,
Hurled wicked taunts at the Lord and criticized him
With his own words and like a bristling goat
He tore at the lovely vine[8] with his poisonous mouth.
The other, worshipping Christ with words of prayer,
Turned away his suffering gaze in dismay, but only his gaze,
For the double set of wounds prevented him moving his hands.
220 He is the one sheep the Lord our shepherd goes out to look
    for
All over the wilderness when it goes astray,[9] and rejoices to
    bring back
With him into your fields, O Paradise, always full of flowers,
Where the grassy meadow spreads its charm and the delightful
    groves
Are nourished by watering streams; amidst the gardens
Striking for their abundant fruits which never fail,
The serpent grumbles that its former inhabitant has returned.
And so each of the robbers undertook a different task
By a different path and both performed a great act of violence.
For the one entered the infernal gates, the other those of
    heaven.
230 The one, making for the depths, penetrated the boundaries of
    hell,
While the other captured the kingdom of heaven by his act of
    plunder.
Then suddenly a horrendous darkness fell,
Taking possession of the whole sky, covering the shadowy
    daylight

With gloomy mourning; the sun buried
Its glistening rays in a cloud, veiled in a dark mantle,
And withdrew, darkening the sad world with its grief.
The elements were granted the right to look upon this face;
Deprived of their father's support, they showed joy at his rising,
Grief at his setting. For as the light shone forth
240 At the time of the Lord's birth, so at his death it withdrew,
Not remaining absent for long, but providing by this period of
    time
A hidden spiritual meaning; for just as for three hours
The darkened stars hid in the unilluminated sky, so for three
    days
The Lord endured imprisonment in the cave that was his tomb.

# PROSPER OF AQUITAINE

## Introduction

The two epigrams and the passage from the poem *De Ingratis* (*On the Ungrateful People*) translated below are taken from the work of Prosper of Aquitaine who was active in the second quarter of the fifth century. From his hand we have not only this long poem and the 106 epigrams on sayings taken from Augustine's works, but also 392 prose sayings from the same source (*Liber sententiarum*), a number of letters, theological works, expositions on the Psalms, a work entitled *De vocatione omnium gentium* (*The Calling of All Nations*) in which the author argues that God wishes all men to be saved, and the *Chronica*, a history of the world. It used to be thought that Prosper was also the author of the *Carmen de Providentia Divina* (*Poem on Divine Providence*), a poem of 972 lines of elegiac couplets and hexameters, in which the problem of providence is discussed in the context of God's creation of the world and in relation to the recent invasions by Vandals and Goths into Gaul, but this attribution is now discredited. Most of Prosper's works are concerned with defending and disseminating Augustine's teachings, especially those on grace and free-will. Gennadius tells us that though Prosper was born in Aquitaine, he moved to Marseilles where he became involved in the semi-Pelagian controversy that erupted around 426 with its epicentre in southern Gaul. After Augustine's death in 430 Prosper continued to work to disseminate Augustine's teachings, transforming them and making them acceptable. He moved to Rome and spent the last years of his life working for Pope Leo the Great.

Prosper's influential work might be admired for the classical quality of its style but despite this, the poetry is rather flat and dull, showing that technical competence is not sufficient to make a poet. His poetry reveals a familiarity with Virgil, Ovid and Lucretius. His epigrams were particularly popular in later years, providing a convenient means for students of learning moral lessons and elements of Augustinian doctrine. It is to these epigrams that Alcuin, for example, refers in his poem on the bishops, kings and saints at York, as existing in the library at York in the eighth century.

The passages selected for translation include two of Prosper's epigrams on themes from Augustine's teaching (one based on a passage from Augustine's *Enarrationes in Psalmos* and the other on a passage from a chapter on the question of whether suicide is ever a mark of greatness of soul, taken from the *City of God*) and an excerpt from the final lines of Prosper's poem *De Ingratis*, directed against Pelagian doctrines, particularly on the questions of sin, grace and free will.

## Texts

Latin text: his works are scattered around volumes 45, 50 and 51 of PL; the epigrams and poem *De Ingratis* are to be found in PL 51; some of his work is now also contained in CCSL 68A (1972).

Example of Latin verse form; elegiac couplets

*Epigram* 77.1–4

Magnum peccatum est amor immoderatus habendi
    Et plus quam vitae sufficiat, cupiens.
Nam quod nos vestit, quod pascit, cura salutis,
    Si vanis sit mens libera, non onerat.

*Epigram* 52 is based on Saying 52 from the *Liber Sententiarum* which is itself an excerpt from Augustine's *City of God* 1.22, part of his discussion of whether suicide can ever be justified in certain circumstances:

> We rightly ascribe greatness to a character who chooses to endure rather than escape from a life of misery and to despise the criticism of his fellow human beings, and especially that of the common people which is often enveloped in a cloud of error, in comparison with the pure light of a clear conscience.

## Epigram 52

He who can lead a life weighed down by misfortunes
And is willing to endure troubles rather than escape from
　　them,
Has a stronger character than one who is afraid
To bear unjust criticism from uneducated people.
A mind that is upright and has a clear conscience
Shines more brightly the more affliction it endures.

*Epigram 77* is based on the prose Saying 80 from the *Liber Sententiarum Augustini*. Saying 80 is a paraphrase of part of Augustine's *Enarratio in Psalmum* 147.12:

We are proved to have much in our possession that is super-
fluous, if we retain only what is necessary. For nothing is
enough for those who seek vain things; and he who possesses
without using them things which would help the poor, has in
some way appropriated what belongs to others.

## Epigram 77

An excessive desire for possession is a great sin,
As is wanting more than is necessary for life,
For what clothes us, feeds us, and our care for our health
Does not weigh us down, if the mind is free from vanities.
And so if there is anything left over which we do not need,
It should be used to benefit the weak and help the needy.
For anyone who out of greed stores up what he does not need to
　　spend,
Is stealing from the poor what he does not give to someone else.

## Carmen de Ingratis 945–997

Let them then be silent who say that one must be careful
That the holy ones are not deprived of an opportunity to win
　　the prize,
If their good qualities are not to be their own.
For those who teach this with excessively arrogant impiety,
Is it not their intention to deprive us of justice and virtue
950 And of God; to prevent light from flashing forth in the
　　night,

What is weak from regaining strength, and what is dead from
    living?
But to drink these things from the highest source
Of what is truly good, and to shine for ever with heavenly
    radiance
Should be our glory; our hope lies not in the flower of the field
    that withers.[1]
For just as the vine branch is unable to produce any fruit
Unless it remains on the vine which helps to bring the sap[2]
From the root into the leaves, and fills the grapes with must,
So those who are barren of virtues and bear no fruit
Will feed the everlasting fires: those who abandon the vine
960  And dare to trust in the immoderate freedom of the foliage
So that their fertility is not dependent on the fruitfulness of
    Christ
And who believe that they can excel by means of their own efforts
Better than if God is the source of the virtues that please him.
And so let them realize that they will be worthless and ugly
When God becomes the sole glory for the holy ones
Who are transformed. No longer will physical hardship oppress
And grind down those who are unsure, but in all things for ever
Christ will be all in all. But if this is lovely and great above all
    things,
Why are they ashamed even in this vale of tears to have their
    powers
970  From God, to have very little of human effort
Because it is nothing but sin which destroys
Freedom and to freedom alone do wicked deeds return?
And yet when we focus our minds on holy acts,
When a chaste mind resists the desires of the flesh,
When we refuse to yield to the tempter and when tormented
By painful punishments, our mind remains unaffected,
Then we are acting with freedom; but with a freedom redeemed
And guided by God who is light from the highest light,
Life, health, virtue, wisdom. It is the grace of Christ that allows
    freedom
980  To run, rejoice, endure, beware, choose, press on,
To have faith, hope, love, to be purified and justified.
For if anything we do is right, O Lord, we do it
With your help; you inspire our hearts, you grant the wishes –
Those you wish to grant – of one who asks; you preserve what
    you bestow,

Create rewards from favours granted, adding prizes to your
    gifts.
But one must not imagine that our efforts can therefore be
    diminished,
Our striving towards virtue relaxed or our mental efforts grow
    dull,
Because the good qualities of holy people are yours and
    whatever
Is healthy and strong in these people depends on you for its
    power;
990 So it might seem that the human will can do nothing, while
    you do all.
For what does the will achieve without you, but to be exiled far
    from you?
The paths are always steep and when the will moves along them
On its own impulse it goes astray unless you in your goodness
    take it up
When it is tired and weak, bring it back, care for it, protect
    and adorn it.
Then it will make rapid progress, its eyes will be clear-sighted,
Its freedom free, its wisdom wise and its justice just,
Strong its virtue and its powers effective.

# CLAUDIUS MARIUS VICTORIUS

## Introduction

According to the literary historian Gennadius, Claudius Marius Victorius (or Victor), the author of the poem entitled *Alethia* (*Truth*), was a rhetor from Marseilles who lived until the second quarter of the fifth century and who wrote a work consisting of four books of commentary in verse on Genesis. In fact, only three books of the poem exist today: as it stands we have a paraphrase of the book of Genesis down to the destruction of Sodom,[1] but it may be that the poem originally continued down to the death of Abraham. Book 1 covers the first three chapters of Genesis, the second book chapters 4–7 and the third book, chapters 8–19. The work now exists in only one manuscript (Par.lat. 7558 from the ninth century)[2] and the printed text, despite the recent work of Hovingh, remains problematic. The author has been highly praised for his poetic abilities,[3] but the style of the poem is abstract and difficult, while Gennadius considered that the author 'expresses thoughts of little value in his poetry'. Evans (1968) suggests that this work was written in order to refute Lucretius' views on man's creation and development. According to the 126-line prayer with which he prefaces his work, the author had a didactic intention in writing and was keen to defend free-will,[4] seeing man as the goal of God's creation. The poet treats the material with greater freedom than, for example, Cyprian the Poet: he amplifies the narrative, adding his own material from various traditions, including paganism and Platonism, and allowing his poetic imagination free rein. Unlike Cyprian, too, Claudius Marius Victorius stresses man's state of guilt after the Fall and indeed his longest digression is the description at the beginning of Book 2 of man's condition after the Fall. Apart from the influence of Lucretius, we can see that of Virgil, Ovid, Lactantius, Prudentius, Ambrose's *Hexaemeron*, and Prosper of Aquitaine who was writing at much the same time and in the same area as Claudius Marius Victorius.

Despite the freshness of the descriptions and the interest of the exegetical material, this poem does not seem to have enjoyed a wide circulation as the paucity of manuscripts and lack of references in other literature confirm. I have selected for translation the passage from Book 1 recounting the serpent's seduction of Eve and God's punishment, and part of the section at the beginning of Book 2 describing Adam and Eve's state after the Fall.

## Texts

Latin texts: CSEL 16 (1888), PL 61, CCSL 128 (1960) ed. Hovingh.

Example of Latin verse form; hexameters

1.1–6

Ante polos caelique diem mundique tenebras,
Ante operum formas vel res vel semina rerum,
Aeternum sine fine retro, sine fine futuri
Esse subest cui semper, erat deus unus, apud quem
Vivebat genitus verbum deus et simul almus
Spiritus, arcani vitalis summa vigoris.

## Alethia 1.398–547

*The serpent addresses Eve*

*Based on Genesis 3*

'O human race, deprived of a better life and unaware
Of good things! For he who cannot distinguish the difference
400 Between the good and its opposite, does not even know what good is.[5]
That is why God refused to allow man to pick the special fruit
In case this should dispel their mental darkness,
Granting them perception and all that is best, while the other side
Of things, teaching them to become skilled in all secrets,
Might make them like the gods.' May I be permitted here to expatiate
A little and to lament our ancestors' disgraceful fall.

119

O how wretched are the pagan peoples, driven by their
    madness
To practise different customs! It is clear in what death the
    profane
Perished utterly. The grim serpent's blasphemous voice
410 Was the first to pronounce the word 'god' in the plural form,
He who then became the cause of death. For after the credulous
    Eve
Had broken the law by means of her sacrilegious bites,
Now well-versed in the evil which she had experienced,
She sought solace for her sin and planned to drag her willing
    husband into crime,
Using the very cunning which had been her downfall. And so,
    overcome
By a twofold enemy, poor Adam surrendered to sin
And tasted the apples whose sacred juiciness made them most
    enticing.
But because in them lay concealed the harsh law's ruling
Which was to bring more than just death through the serpent's
    poison,
420 As soon as they violated their bodies by tasting what was
    forbidden,
They were at once aware of sin, and the crime they had
    committed
Increased, affecting their hearts with a strange feeling.
First they felt fear, then shame; for previously they had been
    allowed
To live naked, unaware of it, whether because as newly-made
    humans
They had hearts full of nourishing energy, conscious of heavenly
    matters,
And focused only on heaven and earth, filled with thoughts
That were always turned to their Father as their model.
They observed the miracles of the divine secrets
By means of the radiance of their almost incorporeal minds;
430 Concern for their bodies had not yet affected them for they
    understood not,
As their souls were better, or because passion could not
    penetrate their bodies
Which would never be weakened by old age with the passing of
    time,
Passion which would make them know all that is necessary.

But when the energy of eternal life had drained from these
    creatures
Who were mortal now, only then did both cold and heat
Alternate in the atmosphere and the humans perceived – oh
    no! –
That they had no clothes, and secretly they blushed
At their own sex. They complained miserably and then, silently
    weeping,
They made new coverings by sewing together leaves
440 From the shady fig tree, coverings which once their bodies were
    clothed
Would strip away the shame filling their minds as a result of
    sin.
But frightened as they were, even this was not enough. What
    should they do,
Where could they escape the crime branded on them, where
    escape themselves?
If only the ground had opened up, they would have loved to
    bury themselves.
So closely related to their punishment was their sin that the
    thought of death
Now pleased them – poor creatures, who had feared mortality.
    They seek a refuge
In the woods and shady groves, the deceptive solace of an
    ineffective hiding-place.
For where are you permitted to conceal your trembling body,
You, Adam, you, I mean who will soon be the first to be
    removed?
450 The Father's living power is present, filling the most remote
    places
Of the world: as it spreads it extends to hidden places far away.
But it is truly sinful for those who are frightened to deceive by
    hiding.
He who flees to the Lord can escape the supreme Lord
In his flight; but if you leave him in your mind alone,
In what vast darkness you are lying without being hidden!
When he calls and asks where you are,[6] he proves both things at
    once.
For why does God seek you when he can see you and since you
    will always
Be present to him? Even death itself cannot remove you from
    him

By its own theft, death which you undergo with a frail mind.
460 Why does he ask where you are, unless because he admits
That you who fell of your own accord to his great grief are not
    with him
And that you have fallen from the sacred heavens?
But the Father's holy love does not permit despair, for his
    mercy –
May it be right for me to say it and also to prove what is said –
Exceeds his justice. He does not so much frighten me with his
    harsh voice
When he asks reprovingly where you are, what you are
    thinking in your fear,
As much as he revives me, because even after the sins
    committed
He calls out, calling back the one who has fallen and hidden
    himself in fear,
And is more or less buried. One need not look far for examples:
470 The very giving of the fault is proof of the Lord's kindness.
After the search had found the guilty ones and brought them out,
The Almighty began to speak – heaven, sea and earth trembled
As he spoke, and as they shook they opened up their vast
    recesses
And created Hell, while he sentenced the guilty pair to
    punishment –
'Since you considered it safe to disobey our orders
And committed a series of crimes without hesitation,
I will sentence those who offended recently with what I regard
    as a just punishment.
Among all the things which we instructed you to enjoy
    throughout the world,
You will be cursed and more so the envious mind which you
    conceal within,
480 You serpent who dispossessed the humans created to enter
    heaven;
You are the origin of harsh death for those you compelled,
By means of your deceit, to touch the forbidden fruits.
So that the punishment might match your crime – O
    horrible! –
You who plunged the human beings to earth will lie stretched
    out
On the hostile soil, while your belly makes a furrow in the hard
    earth.

You used food to make them sin: for such a heinous deed
You, too, will always feed upon the earth's filthy products.
And because you flattered yourself that you were worthy to be
The first inventor of death, you will die by a bloody
    punishment.
490 In particular I shall provoke the hatred of the human race
Against your whole race, imbued as you are with cruel poisons,
And so as to destroy you more effectively, I command that you
    always be feared.
You will exist on a level lower than the feet of this woman
Whom you are proud to have subjected in your first act of
    deceit;
Prostrate on your belly you will lie in wait to attack the soles of
    her feet
In such a way that in her fear she also crushes your head.'
He spoke and then with these words he addressed Eve, who had
    turned pale:
'And you who thought it was no crime at all for the fruit to
    destroy
Yourself alone, you tricked your poor husband with the intention
500 Of harming him and gained control over him by such a terrible
    crime,
You will bear the yoke of a servant and in subjection you will
    endure
Your husband's harsh will and suffer hardships
As a result of unremitting misfortunes, so that you who first
    dared to increase
The crime you had begun, might live amidst many dangers;
In giving birth to one child after another, you will suffer such
    torments
That those mortals whose creation was caused by your sin,
Might cause their mother to die, torn apart in childbirth.
And you, who considered it proper to attach more importance
To feminine wiles than to our warnings and the first bonds of
    salvation,
510 You who dared to die voluntarily, this is the fate you must
    accept for your guilt:
The earth which you plough to create furrows will be cursed
Because of your crimes and when tilled it will bring forth
    menacing
Thorns and thistles and misguided hope will cheat you of what
    you desire.

You failed to persist in serving me faithfully,
And so let the earth fail to keep faith with you. Of your own
    free will
You refused to live happily amidst these delights and to live
For all time: now you must live by hard labour,
Live in misery until creeping old age turns you into earth,
Because that is what you are, and returns you to the earth.'
520 He spoke but then, taking pity on them for not knowing how
    to protect
Their bodies against the weather, he clothed them with animal
    skins
And taught them how to defend their lives. But to prevent
    Adam from daring
To repeat the wrongdoing which he was planning, motivated
    by fear of death,
If at the end of the case, ignorant of things, he were to seek
    from the tree of life
The proud assistance of his original authority, and live
    redeemed by no stratagem
On his father's part and if the mystical order were to vanish
    from the world
And worse things always await those wretched ones in their
    permanently guilty state,
God immediately caused winds to be stirred up in the depths of
    the forest
530 To drive out from the sacred grove those he had ordered to
    depart –
The air holds them fast, carrying them bound together by a
    whirlwind
Which keeps them suspended: the wind takes control of the
    whole lower atmosphere
While nature declines – and when the gusts abate, the winds
    put them down
On the ground, from where their bodies originally came.
They are released from such a great space and free from danger
But not free from sorrow troubling their hearts.
They are upset by the grim comparison between where they
    have ended up,
And what they have lost, between the kind of life they had and
    what will follow.
Their minds perceive a heap of differences and they ponder to
    themselves,

540 Both asking each other, 'How different am I now? How have I
　　　changed?'
　　They are unsure whether to attribute this to their original act of
　　　sin
　　And its punishment, because their error forced them to
　　　understand the power of evil,
　　And whether this is death, or, if more serious things await
　　　them,
　　Whether they will be granted a return, wretched as they are, or
　　　will they
　　Lose for ever what they have left, and whether, since it was on
　　　account of a tree
　　That the path of bitter death opened up for the world and for
　　　future generations,
　　It may be that by means of some tree or other life may yet
　　　return.

## Alethia 2.13–34

*Adam and Eve's first impressions of the world outside paradise*

　　The heights are stiff with jagged rocks, the valleys covered by
　　　forests,
　　The plains are covered with grass, the elevated areas full of
　　　bristling brambles.
　　Alas, with what eyes they look upon this, with what feelings
　　　they see it,
　　They whose minds are full of paradise. Moreover, the reason for
　　　their sorrow
　　Is not simply that there is spread before them a sight now filled
　　With every hardship, but, because they remember the good
　　　things,
　　The beauty of the sacred garden now appears to shine forth
　　　more brightly,
20 　Now its lovely woods produce their riches in greater
　　　abundance,
　　Now its fruits have more delightful benefits and a more
　　　delicious taste,
　　Now the earth breathes forth sweet odours from the living
　　　flowers
　　Rebuking those who are gloomy because of the lack of
　　　fragrance here.

O Paradise, how differently you repay them for what they
    deserve!
Comparison with the inferior things makes you seem all the
    more wonderful
And you cause the only things that remain to the wretches to
    seem even worse.
Here there is no gentle love of life, and the lack of things
Suggests that death might now be welcome to prevent greater
    need
Adding yet greater misfortunes; for a burning desire
30  For food drives them to examine all the foods that might still
    their greed
Produced by the unfruitful trees, forcing them to examine
    unfamiliar plants
With dangerous roots to find some food somewhere:
Hunger itself makes it impossible to escape such a life
Although it drives them to long to escape it.

# PAULINUS OF PELLA

## Introduction

The work known by the Greek title *Eucharisticos (Thanksgiving)*[1] is an autobiographical poem of 616 hexameter lines written to express the author's gratitude for God's protection and guidance, especially in times of misfortune, of which his long life seems to have been full, for the author tells of his own illness as a teenager, his father's death, the problems caused by the barbarian invasions in Gaul[2] in the first half of the fifth century, the death of his wife and his separation from his children. The author was Paulinus of Pella, so-called because he was born in Pella in Greece in the mid-370s where his father was posted as an imperial administrator. As a child, Paulinus moved from Greece to Carthage, thence to Rome, finally ending up in Bordeaux from which his family originally came – in fact, it would seem that his grandfather was the poet Ausonius. The poem is of interest as giving us a picture of someone who first spoke Greek but had to learn Latin and who had first-hand experience of the barbarian invasions, providing fascinating details of the life of a wealthy landowner in the Gaul of the period.

However, the poem seems does not seem to have been widely read during the following centuries and is hardly ever mentioned by later writers. It now exists in only one manuscript, Bern MS 317 from the ninth or tenth century.

In the translated excerpt I have chosen to focus on Paulinus' early life, his childhood, studies and marriage, down to the death of his father.

## Text

Latin text: CSEL 16 (1888), P.H. Evelyn White in the Loeb edition of Ausonius, vol. 2 (1921) with English translation, SC 209 (ed. C. Moussy, Paris 1974) with French translation.

Example of Latin verse form; hexameters

*Eucharistico*s 1–7

Enarrare parans annorum lapsa meorum
Tempora et in seriem deducere gesta dierum,
Ambigua exactos vite quos sorte cucurri,
Te, deus omnipotens, placidus mihi, deprecor, adsis
Adspiransque operi placita tibi coepta secundes,
Effectum scriptis tribuens votisque profectum,
Ut tua te merear percurrere dona iuvante.

## Eucharisticos 22–245

When I was a baby, physically helpless, you gave me strength
To endure the hazards of travel by land and sea,
For though I was born at Pella which had once been the
    cradle
Of King Alexander, not far from Thessalonica's walls,
Where my father was deputy to the illustrious Prefect,
I was entrusted to my nurse's trembling arms
And conveyed to a foreign part of the world, across the sea,
And over snowy ridges and the Alps traversed by torrents,
30  Over the Ocean and the swirling waves of the Tyrrhenian Sea,
Until I came as far as the walls of Phoenician Carthage:
All this, by the time the moon in her monthly orbit
Had replenished her disk with new light for the ninth time
    since my birth.
From there, as I learned, when eighteen months had passed
Under the proconsulship of my father, I was called again
To the sea and the routes we had travelled before, so that I
    might behold
The famous walls of glorious Rome, the world's leading city.
These things were present in my subconscious; with my sense
    of sight
I could not recognize them, but later I learned of them

40    Through the careful telling of those to whom they were
          familiar,
    And decided to include them, bearing in mind the purpose of
          this work.
    At last, when we reached the end of our long journey,
    Arriving in the land of my ancestors, at my grandfather's house,
    I came to Bordeaux, where the lovely river Garonne
    Brings the Ocean's tidal waters inside the city walls,
    Carrying ships through the gate which with its walls
    Even now encloses a spacious harbour within the city.
    Then too, my grandfather who was consul in that same year,
    First became known to me there, before I turned three years
          old.
50    After I turned three I increased in physical energy,
    My feeble limbs grew strong and my mind, aware of its
          faculties,
    Through experience learned to know how things should be
          used.
    And now, as far as I can remember such things, I must relate
    With appropriate honesty, all that needs to be known about me.
    But what else from my childhood years –
    The years which, it seems, could recommend themselves to me
    By their own virtues, of freedom, play and gaiety –
    What should I more gladly recall or more fittingly dare to
          include
    In this little book of mine which I am hammering out in verse,
60    Than my parents' affection and their remarkable hard work.
    They were always good at combining the discipline of my
          education
    With special treats; theirs was a wise concern, exercised with
          due control,
    To instil into me the means of good behaviour
    And to help my untrained mind to make rapid progress –
    To learn, almost along with my first steps in the alphabet,
    To beware the ten special marks of ignorance
    And equally to avoid those vices.
    Although the practice of these disciplines has long fallen into
          disuse,
    No doubt as a result of the moral decline of our age,
70    Yet, I admit, the old Roman practice that I followed
    Pleases me more and makes an old man's life more acceptable.
    Quite early on, by the time I reached the age of five,

I was made to read and learn about the teachings of Socrates,
Homer's tales of war and the wanderings of Ulysses.
And then I was told to read through the works of Virgil, too,
Even though I hardly had a good grasp of the Latin language,
Being used as I was to the conversation of our Greek servants
Whom I had now grown close to, having played with them for
    a long time.
As a result, I admit, it was too hard a task for me, a child,
80  To grasp what was said in these books in a strange tongue.
This bilingual teaching may well be suited to more capable
    minds
And may make those skilled in it appear doubly brilliant,
But the division – too barren, as I now realize –
Easily drained dry my intellect's narrow stream.
Now even against my will this page of mine reveals this,
A rashly-written page, to be sure, which I voluntarily publish
    to be read,
But which I hope will not disgrace me with regard to the
    matters
Of which I am trying to compose a written record.
For my chaste parents, in their solicitous concern,
90  Trained me in this way from childhood, so that I need never fear
That someone's slanderous talk should damage my reputation.
Although this repute, well-earned, retains its lustre,
Yet it would have adorned me then with this more valuable
    honour
If in my early life my parents' hopes had remained consonant
With my own desires in this respect,
And had kept me for ever a child of yours, O Christ,
More rightly making this the focus of their love for me,
That by rejecting for a short time the present attractions of the
    flesh
I might gain everlasting rewards in the world to come.
100  But since I am now obliged to believe that this
Which you have shown was your will, was of greater advantage
    to me,
Almighty everlasting God, you who rule the universe,
By renewing for me, sinful as I am, your life-giving gifts,
I now owe you all the greater thanks on my behalf,
The greater the sins of which I recognized my guilt.
For whatever culpable or unlawful thing I have carelessly
    committed

As I passed without clear directions through life's shifting
    sands,
I know that by your mercy I can be forgiven for everything
Since the time when, condemning my fallen self, I took refuge
    in your laws.
110 If ever I was able to avoid any sins which if committed
Would make me even more guilty than I am,
This too, I am aware, has been granted to me as a gift from God.
But I will return to the sequence of events and to the period
Through which I passed when, absorbed in the study of
    literature,
Of my own accord I seemed to myself already to sense some
Of the desired progress for all the effort I had put in, and was
    glad of it.
Both a Greek and a Latin tutor were putting pressure on me at
    once
And I would perhaps have gained a worthy reward, too,
Had not a severe attack of quartain fever suddenly
120 Put a stop to the successful efforts of my studies
When I had only just reached the fifteenth year of my life.
But since my parents were driven frantic in their love for me,
Seeing that they considered my physical recovery from the
    illness
Was more important than the training of my tongue in
    eloquence,
And as the doctors from the first advised that I should be
    surrounded
By unceasing gaiety and everything pleasing to the mind,
My father was so keen to arrange for this himself
That though he had recently given up hunting, a hobby he had
    loved,
(In fact he had done this solely for the sake of my studies
130 So as not to interfere with them by making me the companion
    in his pastime
And so as not ever to enjoy his hobby alone, without my
    company)
For my sake he took it up again with greater commitment
Devising every means which this sport offered
Whereby I might be able to regain my health, as desired.
These means, long continued through the period of my
    protracted illness,
Introduced in me a distaste for study, a distaste

Which from then on never left me; it persisted afterwards when
    I was well
And damaged me when a new love for the deceitful world
    moved in
And when my parents' over-protective affection receded.
140 It was enough for them to be pleased by my recovery
And as my growth increased, so I went increasingly astray
And readily became established in the pursuit of youthful
    desires:
I wanted a fine horse with splendid trappings,
A tall groom of my own, a swift hunting dog and a handsome
Hawk, a ball decorated with gold and expressly brought from
    Rome
Which was what I needed for our energetic ball games;
I wanted fashionable clothes and regularly to receive
All the latest things, gently perfumed with Arabian myrrh.
Also, when I recall how once my energy returned, I spent my
    time
150 Galloping on my fast horse, and how often I narrowly avoided
Falling headlong from it, then it is right that I should believe
It was by the grace of Christ I was preserved: it is a pity that at
    the time
I was unaware of this, due no doubt to the pressing attractions
    of this world.
Torn between these attractions and my parents' wishes
Which were set on my continuing the family line,
At quite a late stage of my development I became fired with
    lust
And threw myself into the unfamiliar pleasures of youthful
    indulgence
Which, as a child, I used to think I could easily avoid.
However, as far as it was possible to curb and control
160 My self-indulgent behaviour by means of careful restraint,
To stop myself piling more serious offences on my faults
I resisted these temptations by applying this chastening rule:
I must never seek to have sex with anyone against her will
Or belonging to someone else, remembering to preserve my
    self-respect
And avoid sex with free-born girls even if they offered
    themselves willingly;
I must be content to make use of the attractions of the servants
    at home,

Seeing that it was preferable to be guilty of a fault than a crime,
Fearful as I was of incurring any damage to my reputation.
170 I am aware that at that time one son was born to me
But I never set eyes on him then (and he soon died)
Nor did I ever see any illegitimate child of mine
When excessive freedom, allied with the attractions of youth,
Could have taken hold and caused me more serious harm,
If you, O Christ, had not already then been concerned for me.
Such was my life from around my eighteenth year
And it continued thus until I had completed two decades,
When my parents' affectionate concern forced me
Against my will, I admit, to abandon this behaviour whose
     charm
180 I had grown used to, and made me take on a new role as
     husband
To a wife whose property was deemed splendid for its ancient
     name
Rather than for any pleasure possession of it could give
At that time for it brought with it too many problems
Having long been neglected due to the indolence of its aged
     owner.
He was succeeded by his little grandchild who had survived
After her father's death and it was she who later was married to
     me.
But once I had decided to accept the task imposed on me,
As my rational aims were supported by youthful enthusiasm,
After only a few days I became content to practise the pleasures
190 Of the estate I had acquired and I soon forced both myself
And all my workers to replace seductive idleness with
     unfamiliar cares.
Those I could, I inspired by the example of my own hard work,
The others I compelled against their will, applying a master's
     sternness.
And so I pressed on tirelessly in the duties of the position I had
     adopted:
At once I hastened to bring the fallow fields under cultivation
And quickly to devote attention to renewing the exhausted
     vineyards
By using methods I had learned to be reliable.
Furthermore, though many consider this particularly harsh,
By voluntarily paying in full the taxes I owed
200 At the appointed time I quickly earned for myself

A secure leisure to spend later on my own relaxation.
I always valued this too highly and though at first
It was consistent with my nature which had only moderate
    desires
It later became too self-indulgent and divorced from high aims,
When I wanted my house to be equipped with spacious rooms
At all times suited to the different seasons of the year,
My table sumptuous and elegant, my servants numerous and
    young,
The furniture plentiful and attractive for various purposes,
My silver plate outstanding more for its price than for its
    weight,
210 Workmen skilled in different crafts to carry out my orders
    efficiently,
And stables full of horses in good condition,
And also handsome carriages in which I might safely ride.
And yet I was not so much intent on enlarging upon these
As I was keen to preserve them; neither was I over-eager
To increase my wealth nor to seek high office,
But rather, I admit, I was a devotee of luxury,
As long as it could be obtained with the least possible expense
And could continue without damage to my good repute,
Lest the stigma of extravagance should stain my honourable
    pursuits.
220 But though all this was pleasing and welcome to me for my
    enjoyment
It was outweighed by my great affection for my parents, which
    was dearer still,
Binding me to them with the ties of overpowering love,
So that for the greater part of the year I stayed with them,
Devoting myself to their needs, but never longer than they or I
    wished,
And thus both sides benefited and our happiness was mutual.
If only the enjoyment of this life had continued longer,
Granted by Christ's generous gift,
And that the former period of peace had persisted too.
My father's frequent giving of advice
230 Could have helped my youthfulness in many ways
And my training could have progressed, led by his good
    example.
But when the third decade of my life had passed,
Sorrow and cares took over, caused by two tragic events:

For there was general grief at the public disaster
When the enemy poured into the heart of the Roman Empire,
And then came the private sorrow caused by my father's death:
For the last days of the end of his life
Were more or less continuous with the days when peace was
    broken.
But for me the damage inflicted on my home by the ravaging
    enemy,
240 Great though it was in itself, was far less severe
When compared with the immoderate grief at my father's
    death,
He who had made both home and country dear to me.
For by performing kindnesses to each other, inspired
By genuine affection, we lived with such closeness
That our harmony surpassed that of friends who are the same
    age.

# DE LIGNO CRUCIS

## Introduction

The poem of 69 lines which is translated below in its entirety is sometimes referred to as the *De Ligno Crucis* (*The Tree of the Cross*), sometimes as *De Pascha* (*On Easter*) and sometimes as *De Ligno Vitae* (*The Tree of Life*).[1] Equally confusing is the fact that it has been variously attributed to Tertullian, Cyprian and a certain Victorinus (sometimes thought to be identical with the rhetor Marius Victorinus mentioned in Augustine's *Confessions*). It is often printed alongside some other poems of less than 500 lines whose attribution is equally uncertain: poems on Sodom, on Jonah, on the judgement of God and on the resurrection of the dead.

The poem presents us with a neat allegorical description of a tree representing the cross on which Christ was crucified. The tree grows up from a stem (reminiscent of the rod of Jesse in the Old Testament)[2] and produces health-giving fruits, destined to benefit not the local inhabitants (i.e. the Jews) but foreign peoples (the Gentiles). Beneath the tree is a spring of clear water, representing the waters of baptism, in which those who wish to pick the fruit of the tree must wash before they may eat of the fruit that brings salvation. The poem contains much numerological symbolism, alluding for example to the twelve disciples, the three days in which Christ remained in the tomb, to the forty days between Easter and Christ's ascension and the fifty days between Easter and the coming of the Holy Spirit at Pentecost. With its central picture of the tree and the spring to which people are drawn, the poet attempts to convey the belief that Christ, by dying on the cross, brings salvation to all who come to him in faith.

The language of the poem is unobtrusively Virgilian, but the poem's descriptions and the use of allegory mean that it resembles Lactantius' *Phoenix*.

**Text**

Latin text: CSEL 3 in the appendix to the works of Cyprian, pp. 305–8; PL 2 in Appendix 1 to the works of Tertullian, col. 1113.

Example of the Latin verse form; hexameters

Lines 1–4

Est locus ex omni medius, quem cernimus, orbe,
Golgotha Judaei patrio cognomine dicunt:
Hic ego de sterili succisum robore lignum
Plantatum memini fructus genuisse salubres.

**The Tree of the Cross**

There is a place, we believe, at the centre of the world,
Called Golgotha by the Jews in their native tongue.
Here was planted a tree cut from a barren stump:
This tree, I remember hearing, produced wholesome fruits,
But it did not bear these fruits for those who had settled there;
It was foreigners who picked these lovely fruits.
This is what the tree looked like: it rose from a single stem
And then extended its arms into two branches
Just like the heavy yardarms on which billowing sails are
    stretched
10 Or like the yoke beneath which two oxen are put to the plough.
The shoot that sprung from the first ripe seed
Germinated in the earth and then, miraculously,
On the third day it produced a branch once more,
Terrifying to the earth and to those above, but rich in life-
    giving fruit.
But over the next forty days it increased in strength,
Growing into a huge tree which touched the heavens
With its topmost branches and then hid its sacred head on
    high.
In the meantime it produced twelve branches of enormous
Weight and stretched forth, spreading them over the whole
    world:
20 They were to bring nourishment and eternal life to all
The nations and to teach them that death can die.
And then after a further fifty days had passed

From its very top the tree caused a draught of divine nectar
To flow into its branches, a breeze of the heavenly spirit.
All over the tree the leaves were dripping with sweet dew.
And look! Beneath the branches' shady cover
There was a spring, with waters bright and clear
For there was nothing there to disturb the calm. Around it in
    the grass
A variety of flowers shone forth in bright colours.
30  Around this spring countless races and peoples gathered,
Of different stock, sex, age and rank,
Married and unmarried, widows, young married women,
Babies, children and men, both young and old.
When they saw the branches here bending down, under the
    weight
Of many sorts of fruit, they gleefully reached out with greedy
    hands
To touch the fruits dripping with heavenly nectar.
But they could not pick them with their eager hands
Until they had wiped off the dirt and filthy traces
Of their former life, washing their bodies in the holy spring.
40  And so they strolled around on the soft grass for some time
And looked up at the fruits hanging from the tall tree.
If they ate the shells that fell from those branches
And the sweet greenery dripping with plenty of nectar,
Then they were overcome with a desire to pick the real fruit.
And when their mouths first experienced the heavenly taste,
Their minds were transformed and their greedy impulses
Began to disappear; by the sweet taste they knew the man.
We have seen that an unusual taste or the poison of gall
Mixed with honey causes annoyance in many:
50  They rejected what tasted good because they were confused
And did not like what they had eagerly grabbed at,
Finally spitting out the taste of what they had for long drunk
    unwisely.
But it often happens that many, once their thoughts are set to
    rights,
Find their sick minds restored and achieve what they denied
Was possible and so obtain the fruits of their labours.
Many, too, having dared to touch the sacred waters,
Have suddenly departed, slipping back again
To roll around in the same mixture of mud and filth.
But others, faithfully carrying the truth within them, receive it

60  With their whole soul and store it deep in their hearts.
And so the seventh day sets those who can approach
The sacred spring beside the waters they longed for,
And they dip their bodies that have been fasting.
Only so do they rid themselves of the filth of their thoughts
And the stains of their former life, bringing back from death
Souls that are pure and shining, destined for heaven's light.

# ORIENTIUS

## Introduction

It would seem that Orientius[1] was writing in Gaul around the years 430–440; the fact that he quotes three lines of the *Carmen de Providentia Divina*, now dated to about 416, means that he cannot have written his poem before then. It has plausibly been suggested that he was Bishop of Auch at that time, of whom three biographies exist. His work of moral instruction, the *Commonitorium*, now exists in a single manuscript (Paris, Bibl.nat.nouv.acq.lat.457). It comprises 518 elegiac couplets divided into two books, the subject of which is an exhortation to lead a Christian life combined with advice on how to win the prize of eternal life, by eschewing such vices as lust, envy, greed, pride, falsehood, gluttony and drunkenness, all of which Orientius depicts in a lively manner. He stresses the dual aspect of human life, divided between a brief earthly life and the more important everlasting heavenly life on which mankind should focus.

Although Venantius Fortunatus mentions this author in his *Life of St Martin*, and the eighth-century writer Paulus Diaconus quotes from the work, it does not seem that Orientius' poem was widely known during the Middle Ages. In modern times, too, it has been undeservedly neglected: although Orientius' verse does not display a high standard of technical competence, the poet speaks with an attractive warmth and directness in a style not overburdened by rhetoric or allusion to earlier authors. From the point of view of the content the poem contains many original and interesting details, such as the list the poet gives in Book 1 of the delights of this life which God has granted (1.117–164) or the references to the contemporary barbarian invasions (2.165–202); from the point of view of style it contains such elements as gnomic moral statements and word play which may be regarded as more typical of medieval than classical poetry.

In the passage translated below the poet warns the reader not to indulge in drunkenness, giving a vivid picture of the physical effects of inebriation.

## Text

Latin text: PL 61, CSEL 16 (1881).

Example of Latin verse form; elegiac couplets

1.111–116

Qui tribuit vitam, largitur commoda vitae,
   Omnibus ut tibi sit praedita deliciis.
Ecce tibi caelum pendet, tibi terra recedit,
   Aera librantur, fluctuat oceanus.
Noctes atque dies succedunt mensibus anni,
   Sol splendet, lucent sidera, luna rubet.

## Commonitorium 2.51–92

*On drunkenness*

I particularly abhor the flooding of the veins with large
      quantities
Of wine, in case the wine should quickly turn to poison.
Just as whenever the dry earth thirsts in times of excessive heat,
– The earth which the skilful farmer is preparing so it might
      bear fruit –
If the thick clouds have moistened the soaking days
Before the sun destroys the weeds that have been rooted out
Then the earth will produce thorns and tares harmful to the
      harvest,
Fruitful in the wrong way, and the seeds will be choked.
In the same way bodies which are given to much wine
60  Come to nothing in their plans and indulge in vices to excess.
Will there ever be anything more sordid, more disgusting
Than if drunkenness should steal you from yourself?
Your head wobbles this way and that and you totter as you
      walk,
Your mind refuses to comprehend, your tongue to produce a
      sound,

Your eyelids close, drooping and heavy with sleep,
You do not know what you are doing, even while you are doing
    it.
What should I say of the heat affecting your reeking face
And your words, all disconnected and jumbled up,
The cups which slip from your hands and the way the food
70  Mixed with wine is often regurgitated all over the tables,
And how your dizzy head leads you through innumerable
    emotions
So you are either laughing or crying hysterically;
And how one minute your drooping limbs revolve in a dance,
The next you are embracing the lascivious dancers?
You like to shout out when you are overwhelmed by food and
    wine,
And perhaps you have even forgotten your own name,
And that of him who generously gives you such things,
When a pious desire to pray to God steals over you.
How many poor people could God feed with what all that cost,
80  How many days of happiness could this one day give?
But while you are now stuffed, the poor man wanders hungry;
You vomit up wine while he hardly has any water to drink.
And if by chance a beggar addresses you, asking for bread, you
    will refuse
To give to those who have nothing, what you have in surplus.
I perceive, reader, that after being quiet for a time you are
    saying
'That is true but what you command is hard';
We are commanded to do hard things: do not imagine that it is
    possible
To climb from earth to heaven without a lot of effort.
It is a great undertaking; but the reward for it is great.
90  He who hopes for the prize should avoid idleness.
No one wins the prize unless he first puts in the effort.
The attractive prize is only given to the winner.

# DRACONTIUS

## Introduction

Blossius Aemilius Dracontius was trained in classical rhetoric at Carthage and then worked as a lawyer there at the end of the fifth century. He was apparently thrown into prison by the Vandal king Guntamund for addressing a poem to the Byzantine emperor Zeno. While in prison Dracontius wrote a poem called the *Satisfactio* in which he admits his guilt and pleads for forgiveness. It was about this time that he also wrote his major work, the *De Laudibus Dei* (sometimes referred to as the *Carmen de Deo*) which consists of 2327 hexameters divided into three books, in which the author praises God the creator and benefactor of mankind. The first book is largely a paraphrase of the account in Genesis of the six days of creation, but it is markedly different from the treatments of such poets as Cyprian, Avitus and Claudius Marius Victorius: the narrative passages are punctuated not so much by allegorical interpretations as by lyrical passages celebrating God's goodness or giving examples of his benevolence, as in the attempt to prove the concept of resurrection by presenting examples of rebirth and regeneration from nature. The second book describes man's sinfulness – a section which allows the poet to verge on the satirical – and God's punishment of man and his mercy towards him, particularly in sending Christ to redeem mankind. This leads to a section recounting the incarnation, passion and resurrection of Christ, as well as an account of some of Christ's miracles. The final book is concerned to show that people should demonstrate their love and faith by sacrificing themselves to God, as Christ sacrificed himself for us. Dracontius gives examples of such self-sacrifice from the Old Testament but also provides a long series (lines 256–530) of heroes and heroines from the legends of antiquity[1] to convince those who are not Christians of the truth of what he is saying. On the whole, his poem is less dependent on Scripture, drawing also on the poet's observations of natural phenomena as well as his knowledge of Christian and classical writings.

Dracontius is a very competent and interesting author who has been unfortunately neglected. His work shows evidence of his familiarity with Virgil,[2] Ovid, Lucan, Statius and Juvenal (for example at 3.745 he quotes the phrase 'mens sana in corpore sano' from Juvenal 10.356), but it is no mere imitation of his literary predecessors but a rich and imaginative exploration of the nature of human existence.

Many manuscripts exist that contain only the first book of the *De Laudibus Dei*, usually shorn of its first 117 lines of introductory praise of God and his goodness to mankind. This is the result of the recension made by Eugenius of Toledo (himself a poet) in the seventh century: in this form the work circulated separately often under the title *Hexaemeron* and was popular throughout the Middle Ages. Arevalo was the first to publish all three books of the work.

**Text**

Latin text: MGH AA 14 (1905), Budé edition (C. Moussy and C. Camus (eds), Paris 1985).

Example of Latin verse form; hexameters

1.1–4

Qui cupit iratum placidumve scire Tonantem,
Hoc carmen, sed mente legat, dum voce recenset.
Agnoscet quem templa poli, quem moenia caeli
Auctorem confessa suum veneranter adorent.

**De Laudibus Dei 1.562–695**

God alone is ruler and creator everlasting,
God is the threefold power, God is wholly three and one,[3]
He who grants each good thing one hopes for,
Never cheating the pure soul of what it confidently expects;
His words never fail to produce immediate results.
In his presence silent hearts can speak through their feelings;
Though the tongue says nothing its words resound above the
  heavens:
The pure soul can entreat God better than the tongue.

570 And so, mindful of his creation, God ordered both the humans
Who had left their peaceful home, to take charge of the world[4]
And to hold everything the world contains under their
    jurisdiction.
That the earth produces flowers and green grass grows,
That ears of wheat form, and trees bear fruit,
That buds sprout from the vines, and trees have lovely locks of
    leaves,
That streams produce rivers, and the sea rises in billows,
That the waves draw the ocean waters and beat upon the shores,
That gusting winds roar and ruffle the shifting seas,
What the earth brings forth – or fire, air, or water –
580 All this was ordered to exist for the use of mankind
So that he who was created from dust, in the image of Christ,
Should rule over all these things and all physical beings
Should submissively serve these creatures clothed in flesh.
There is, however, an incorporeal breath serving man: the wind.
The wind dispels the clouds or the air thickens,
Condensing into clouds; so the rain comes and then clear skies.
The wind nourishes the fruits, the wind forms ears of corn
Which the gentle breeze of summer fans with its breath.
It sheds the blossom to form the fruit, shaking flowers from the
    trees.
590 It kindles the flames with its breath and tempers summer's
    heat.
As it is breathed in and out, life's manifestations continue:
The breath departs and returns in repeated exhalation
And when the air rushes back in, the lungs' lobes breathe it
    out.
The air passes in through the nose, out through the throat, back
    and forth,
Inspiring with life the vital feelings throughout the warm
    limbs;
The lips over which cold air passed just now
Become animated by warm breath which has travelled through
    the throat.
To breathe in this way is not granted to the human body alone:
In all animate beings the air moves in and out.
600 The spirit of God, encompassing all things, sets all bodies in
    motion,
Stirs them up, nurtures, ingrafts them, drives them on.
From it all the different seeds of things derive their origin, too.

Coming out of boundless chaos, in an everlasting stream
They pour forth, formed by the hand of the Creator
And all arranged in order: the gift of creation stands firm for
  ever,
And though they die each day as a condition of existence, they
  do not die.
Who would deny that a rippling river flows from a spring?
And yet the river's source never expects to see its return.
Although it pours forth its waters in full spate without cease,
610 Yet the river's flow denies that it experiences any loss.
Everyone is in the habit of taking flames from flames
But the fire is not diminished when the fire is removed.
One person's profit is often another person's loss,
But who suffers loss from such gains? When the flame
Is removed from the fire, does the fire perhaps lose its radiance?
In creating offspring, physical creatures are not diminished.
Look how God, King and Creator, has granted man more than
  himself:
God in his power created a single man, a single woman,
But one man can create many children; his plentiful offspring
620 Will live on though the race springs from an insignificant
  source.
For God to make birth follow on death would have been
  nothing special,
Had he not allowed life to rise once more[5] after ages had passed.
But in case those who profane the holy laws
Should have the fixed idea that the buried cannot return,
Let them consider the crops in the fields: they spring up again
  every year
After dying in the furrows made by the plough that cleaves the
  earth.
A tree that rises up from roots that have been cut grows taller
And year after year it turns green in its leafy clothing.
Once more the shoots clothe the stems of the grape-bearing
  vine
630 And on the rose bush the red buds return,
And new fruits again burst forth from the fragrant bark:
Their life is fleeting, for age comes upon them as they flower.
Grass, too, comes back to life, with a fresh crop of green hair.
All the trees are reborn and start to sprout anew:
Recently a shoot, now a chopped-down tree, it will in turn
  produce a shoot.

The scaly snake with its star-like markings slips from its skin:
When the skin grows again, its youth returns once more
And the gaping snake slithers off, opening its throat to hiss.
The deer with branches on their heads lose their antlers
640 But when they have eaten snakes their antlers soon sprout again.
The birds of the sky lose their old feathers and are stripped bare
But then fresh plumage begins to cover them, restored once
    more.
Moreover the eyes long dead of the unseeing,
Once the cloud of darkness is dispelled and light returns,
Have regained their sight, and the death mask of the blind
    man's face
Having endured days as dark as night, is made to see.
Does it not often happen that a man half-alive, half-dead,
Lies there bemoaning his living death, his corpse alive in death,
And without death deprived of life in a living death?
650 But his health is restored and revives as the heat returns
To his limbs and a feeling of warmth re-enters his vital organs
Holding his bones firm, quickening his pulse, restoring the sap
    to his marrow.
God renews the lost youth of the phoenix by means of fire:
In old age it burns up completely, then flies from the tomb in
    its prime:
The pyre that destroys its body gives it a body without
    undergoing burial.
The fire has gone out but the flame, already dead, leaps up
    again,
And the devouring fire returns, blazing with its light revived.
A spark flying up can cause a huge fire to start again;
What was smoke is now the whistling steam of the bright fire.
660 As the fire spreads, the crest of the flames grows red, the fire
    licks the air.
The ash that was extinguished when the embers were cold and
    dead
Floats up on high, restless, its hair standing on end.
At daybreak the night dies and fades away, and the golden
    moon vanishes
But as it waxes in its successive risings it collects up its fires
And though invisible, it secretly restores its light and shines
    forth once more.
Its chilly beams, a reflection of the sun, give a false impression
    of day.

On Lucifer's return, the stars in the heavens also die.
Messenger of dawn, carried off by death each day,
Lucifer rekindles its extinguished flames from the stars
670 And the nightly rider flashes forth his brightness from the
     glittering fire.
The dewy dawn spreading purple and pink all over the world
Brings in the day which night's shadows will destroy.
And yet blushing dawn herself dies, falling victim to the sun
     that sent her.
The sun himself, the eye of heaven, servant of the Lord of
     Thunder above the stars,
The sun himself, whose immense fires would cause the
     constellations to wane
Were they not revived in the cool waters of the blue seas,
The sun himself sets; as he slips into the Ocean, the day
     plunges into the waves
And disappears, but in the morning he rises anew from the sea.
As night reaches its own evening, nature lifts up the sun,
     glowing red,
680 From out of the purple waters and then each day
It gives back its treasure for burial during the night,
But at dawn it rises again from the waves, its orb restored.
Persuaded by all these examples we must believe
That what has died is born again by God's power which created
     all things:
Brought to life they grow strong, nurtured by the Lord of
     Thunder
Who although he inhabits the lofty kingdoms of the starry sky
Gives limits to the air, supports the earth, lets the seas flow
And holds in one hand all that his Word created,
An everlasting gift from God, which a single command from
     him could destroy.
690 He is as good as it is proper for the Almighty to be;
All his power he exercises perfectly except his anger and power
     to punish,
But that is as he wants it for he is in essence good and kind and
     loving.
It is not sacrificial offerings that please him but the purity of
     the human soul[6]
Or if the guilty with their wicked desires repent of their crime
And experience a change of heart, becoming pious souls.

# AVITUS

## Introduction

Alcimus Avitus was Bishop of Vienne in southern Gaul from 494–518, in which capacity he devoted his energies to ridding the Church of Arian and Pelagian beliefs. Arianism was particularly strong in this area because the Burgundians who controlled it at the time had accepted Christianity in its Arian form. Gregory of Tours, who tells us of Avitus' efforts, relates that King Gundobad considered abandoning Arianism, under the influence of Avitus' arguments, but was never able to confess in public that the three persons of the Trinity are equal.

Avitus's most famous work is his verse work *De spiritalis historiae gestis* (*The Events of Spiritual History*) in six books, but he was also the author of a dialogue against the Arians and a work written to combat the heresy of Eutyches, as well as 86 extant letters and 34, mostly fragmentary, homilies. His verse work comprises five books based on texts from Genesis and Exodus, relating the Creation, the Fall, the Flood and the crossing of the Red Sea, and a sixth book of 666 hexameters entitled *De consolatoria castitatis laude* (*A Work of Consolation in Praise of Chastity*) addressed to his younger sister Fuscina whom he praises and consoles for her decision to devote herself to a life of chastity instead of choosing marriage and motherhood.

In the five books of the poem *De spiritalis historiae gestis* Avitus is concerned above all to praise Christ and his redemptive work, even though he is telling the story of Adam, Noah and Moses. He does so by treating his material in a typological manner similar to that used by Sedulius, selecting those episodes germane to his purpose and amplifying the chosen texts[1] in a restrained way to draw out the spiritual value of events in the early chapters of the Old Testament and to

149

show how they connect with their fulfilment in the events recounted in the Gospels. Following St Paul,[2] Avitus stresses the links between Adam and Christ, in that Christ, the second Adam, restored to humanity the state of grace which Adam had lost by his actions in paradise. He also sees connections between the Flood and the crossing of the Red Sea in Genesis and the centrality of baptism under the new covenant, which washes away mankind's sins. Thus, within the story of the Creation, the Fall, the Flood and the escape from Egypt, Avitus is able typologically to cover the fundamental points of Christian salvation.

We can see evidence of Avitus' concern to stamp out Arianism and Pelagianism in this poem, the first in his emphasis on the unity of the divine and human natures in Christ, as is particularly clear in Book 3 (362–425) and at the end of Book 4, the second in his emphasis on the guilt incurred by Adam and Eve and its consequences for mankind.

Avitus is a skilful poet with excellent dramatic powers. In his depiction of the Fall, he anticipates Milton in associating Satan with the serpent and his characterization of Satan, together with the addition of Satan's monologue when he is coming to the decision to cause the downfall of the first human beings, is almost as powerful as the parallel episode in *Paradise Lost* (4.32–113).

Much less critical attention has been paid to his poem for his sister in which the poet provides us with many interesting details about women's lives around the year 500, about family life, marriage and motherhood. If the main subject is the popular one in Christian circles of the superiority of virginity over marriage, it is here treated in a more personal way than in most other texts of Late Antiquity. Avitus encourages his sister in her undertaking but also warns her of the dangers involved, in a manner similar to that of Jerome in his famous letter to Eustochium (*Letter* 22). He portrays his sister as a spiritual warrior who should model herself on the Old Testament heroine, Deborah: in this context he refers explicitly to Prudentius' *Psychomachia*. He warns her that virginity is not enough – the true Christian must also be free from other sins; in an interesting extended metaphor he uses words connected with sexual sin and pregnancy to apply to the mind. Below is included the passage in which Avitus speaks of the unpleasant aspects of marriage for women and the dangers of childbearing.

## Texts

Latin text: PL 59, MGH AA 6.2 (1883), Books 1–3 ed. D.J. Nodes (Toronto 1985), Books 1–3 (ed. N. Hecquet-Noti, SC 444, Paris 1999).

Example of Latin verse form; hexameters

1.1–8

Quidquid agit varios humana in gente labores,
Unde brevem carpunt mortalia tempora vitam,
Vel quod polluti vitiantur origine mores,
Quos aliena premunt priscorum facta parentum,
Addatur quamquam nostra de parte reatus,
Quod tamen amisso dudum peccatur honore,
Adscribam tibi, prime pater, qui semine mortis
Tollis succiduae vitalia germina proli.

## De Spiritalis Historiae Gestis 1.144–250

*God's creation of Eve, the marriage of Adam and Eve and the creation of paradise*

Meanwhile the sixth evening brought back the beginning of
   night,
Driving away the light with the alternation of the times of day.
As all living things sought welcome rest,
Adam settled down to sleep, his limbs relaxed.
The Almighty Father induced in him a deep slumber
That overwhelmed him, dulling his senses with a great
   heaviness
150 So that no force could awaken his soundly sleeping mind.
Even if a loud crash had happened to strike his untroubled ears,
If the sky had thundered forth and the heavens shaken,
Under the weight of God's hand his body's rest would not have
   been disturbed.
Then from among all his bones God chose a single rib
From the left side and then repaired the damage to the body.
From it he creates a delightful figure, tall and beautiful,
And suddenly those new features develop into a woman
Whom God joins to her husband in an everlasting contract,

Rewarding him with marriage as compensation for his lost rib.
160 That death which Christ chose to undergo
When he assumed a body, followed the model of Adam's sleep:
When Christ was about to suffer and was hanging aloft,
Fastened high on the cross, paying for the sins of the world,
An attendant stuck his spear into Christ's side as he was
　　　stretched out there.
At once, water sprang forth, gushing out of the wound,
Already at that time promising the people a life-giving
　　　purification;
A stream of blood flowed too, providing a sign of martyrdom.
Then while he lay dead for two nights, the Church arose
From the rib in Christ's side, becoming his bride as he slept.
170 In the beginning the Ruler, taking care to sanctify what was
　　　the type
For this important union, joined them in marriage with these
　　　words:
'Live in harmony and devotion to each other and fill the world;
May your offspring live long and increase from this prosperous
　　　seed;
Let the years of their lives be without number or limit.
I grant you generations without end[3] which you will receive
For all time, you who are set as the prime source of your race.
May your great-grandson, scattering through the ages his own
　　　grandsons,
Number his great-grandparents among the living and may his
　　　children's
Children lead their long-lived offspring before their ancestors'
　　　eyes.
180 Then will the law of marriage be respected for all time
And preserved inviolate by all according to its own form.
Let woman, taken from within the man's body, continue
Faithful in marriage and may no one else separate
What God has joined and united: may the husband
Bound by a lawful love, leave his mother and father.
Concern for his parents must not cause these ties to rupture
But the two of them should live together as one flesh.'
In this way God united them in marriage with an everlasting
　　　contract
And announced the wedding festivities, while the angels' song
190 With its harmonious melody rang in celebration of their chaste
　　　modesty.

Paradise was their bridal chamber; the world was given
As the wedding-gift and the stars rejoiced with flames of joy.
There is a place on the eastern edge of the world
Preserved for your mysteries, Nature, where the dawn, born
From the sun's rising, strikes the neighbouring Indians.
Here there lives a people beneath the heavens' blazing sky,
A people darkened by the burning radiance of the bright
    atmosphere.
Upon these people there always falls a pure light; because the
    sky is close,
Their blackened bodies preserve the colour of night with which
    they are born.
200  And yet their eyes shining forth in their dark-skinned bodies,
Sparkle with a stolen brightness and because of their glistening
    eyes
The terror they inspire is all the greater.
Their unkempt hair is stiff: it is pulled back from the receding
    hairline
So that the forehead is bare and free from hair.
But every valuable product that is imported for our use
Was given to this people by nature from the rich earth;
Every fragrant and beautiful product comes from that place.
Here a shoot, the same colour as these people, grows up
From the trunk of the pitch-black ebony; here, too, the ugly
    beast
210  That gives the world the gift of ivory, lays down its lovely
    tusks.[4]
And so passing beyond the Indies to the edge of the world
Where they say that the earth joined its borders to the sky,
There still exists a garden, an enclosed area barred to all mortals
And fenced off with a permanent boundary
After the perpetrator of the original sin fell and was expelled.
The guilty pair were banished from their happy home as they
    deserved,
And then this sacred place acquired heavenly guardians.
Here winter's frosts never come with the alternation of the
    seasons
Nor do the suns of summer ever return after the cold,
220  When heaven's orbit brings back the hot season of the year,
Nor do the fields grow white with frost as the ice thickens.
Here spring is continuous,[5] preserved by the mildness of the
    weather:

No blustery south wind blows here and beneath the cloudless
    sky
The clouds always scatter, yielding to the unbroken spell of
    sunshine.
Nor does the nature of the place demand showers that belong
    not here:
The plants are content to be provided with their own dew.
All the ground is permanently green and the warm earth's
Lovely face is permanently bright; the hills are ever thick with
    grass,
The trees with leaves and they blossom with abundant flowers
230  And strengthen their shoots with fast-flowing sap.
For all that is produced for us now in the course of the year,
Is there produced as ripe fruit within a month.
Lilies shine translucent and never wither in the sun;
The sun's touch never violates the violets and the red roses
Are preserved by grace, suffusing their undying faces.
And so since there is no winter and no parching summer heat,
Autumn fills the year with fruits, spring fills it with its flowers.
Here is produced cinnamon which tradition wrongly has it
Is given to the Arabians, cinnamon which the long-lived bird[6]
    collects
240  When it dies in a death which is its birth, consumed in its nest;
Succeeding itself it rises again by way of the death it sought
And not content with being born just once in the normal way,
The long life of its feeble body is renewed
And repeated beginnings revive the old age which has been
    consumed.
There exists a branch that exudes a fragrant balsam,
Producing a continuous flow from its rich trunk.
Then if by chance a light wind stirs its breath,
The rich woods set in motion by a gentle breeze whisper
At the trembling of their leaves and wholesome flowers
250  Which are scattered on the ground, giving off a lovely
    fragrance.


## 2.35–116

*Satan's decision to avenge his downfall by destroying man*

By means of these benefits the sanctity of their origin kept in
    check

The thoughts of the first created beings, until in the first
    contest
Sin overcame them, overpowered by the treacherous foe.
He had formerly been an angel but later he became inflamed
By his own crime and burned to commit arrogant and
    audacious deeds,
40  Believing that he had made himself and that he was his own
Creator:[7] in his fury his heart was filled with madness:
Denying his creator, he said, 'I shall acquire the title of god
And shall establish my eternal throne above the heavens,
And I shall be like the Most High and equal in supreme power.'
As he made this boastful speech the highest power hurled him
From heaven and then stripped him of his former privilege.
He who was first in order of rank among creatures
Will be the first to be punished at the coming of the Judge,
Since a more severe penalty punishes the one whose downfall
50  Might seem to you amazing, for the perpetrator
Aggravates his crime: there is less guilt when someone
    unknown sins;
The greater the sinner, the more serious his crime is
    considered.[8]
But insofar as his keen intellect penetrates hidden matters,
Sees the future and unlocks the secrets of the world,
The force and vigour of his angelic nature remain.
It is a portent terrible to describe and indicated by remarkable
    signs:
Whatever ghastly deed is committed anywhere in the world,
It is he who instructs the hand of crime and guides its weapons;
It is he, a criminal concealed, who strikes by means of crimes
    visible to all.
60  Often he turns himself into the shape of men
Or of wild beasts, deceitfully changing into new guises.
Sometimes he takes on the false semblance of a flying bird
And then once again puts on a respectable appearance.
He even appears as a young girl with a beautiful body
Attracting passionate looks at the filthy pleasures he offers.
Often, too, he shines forth to the greedy as large amounts of
    silver
Inflaming their thoughts with a desire for counterfeit gold
But disappears when touched by those he has tricked with an
    empty mirage.
In none of his guises can one trust or find lasting beauty:

70   In whatever way he seduces and holds someone to do him harm,
     He masks his face and assumes an external form
     Suited to treachery and appropriate for secret deceit.
     A still greater power had been granted to this cruel creature –
     The power to make himself holy: the nature earlier bestowed
     On this creature was still in force, created good by the Creator,
     But afterwards the rebel wickedly perverted it.
     As soon as Satan saw the newly created humans in their
          peaceful home,
     Leading a life of happiness, free from danger, saw them
          wielding authority
     Over the world which served them according to the law given
          to them,
80   And enjoying all that was subject to them amid tranquil
          delights,
     A spark of jealousy kindled a sudden passion
     And as his envy became inflamed it grew into a raging blaze.
     At that time it was not long since he had fallen from heaven,
     Dragging headlong with him his band of followers.
     Reflecting on this and suppressing the outrage of his recent fall
     He felt more aggrieved at having lost what another possessed.
     Then shame combined with bitterness elicited these complaints
     From his heart and he sighed deeply as he spoke thus:
     'Alas, that this upstart creature should rise up in our place
90   And that this hateful race should be born from our downfall.
     Virtue held me on high, but now look at me! Rejected,
     I am cast out and a thing of clay succeeds to my angelic status.
     Earth possesses heaven, and clay supported on a feeble structure
     Now reigns; my power, transferred to another, is lost to me.
     Yet not completely lost: a large part retains its special strength
     And is renowned for its great capacity to harm.
     I do not wish to delay: already now I am prepared
     To engage in a polite battle, while their early well-being and
          innocent leisure,
     Never having experienced deceit, is vulnerable to my weapons.
100  They will more easily be trapped by treachery while alone
     Before they bring forth abundant offspring for all ages to come.
     Nothing immortal is to be allowed to come forth from the
          earth;
     Let this race be destroyed at its source; the exile of its defeated
          leader
     Will be the seed of its death. Let life at its very beginning

Give birth to the hazards of death; may all die in this one
    person.
Let the root be destroyed so it cannot produce a living plant.
This consolation alone remains to me now in my exile:
If I cannot ascend again to the heavens whose gates are barred
    to me,
Let them also be barred to these people. My fall will be more
    bearable
110 If the new creation is destroyed by means of a similar
    misfortune.
May it share in my destruction, may it participate in my
    punishment
And let it share with me the flames I even now foresee.
But it will not be hard to find an opportunity to deceive them:
I must show them the path I chose to take some time ago
When I fell headlong; the same pride that banished me
From the kingdom will drive man from the gates of paradise.

## A work of consolation to his sister Fuscina 163–204

*The horrors of marriage and motherhood*

You will not grieve for the loss of your children, the proofs of
    your fruitfulness,
Nor will you fear to survive as a widow the husband you
    thought would live for ever:
You will be free from misfortune and will not be affected by the
    sentence
Imposed on Eve, the mother of offspring and of death,
Who brought forth a child that was killed,[9] while the
    punishment lived on.
A woman subject to her husband has to bear him as master of
    their marriage:
Enduring wedlock she is just a slave in a disgusting bed;
170 She is but a captive of the bed, bearing the empty name of wife,
And called her husband's consort in a hollow charade,
Oppressed by the yoke, forced to bear an unequal burden on her
    own.
When ten months have brought continuous sickness
And her stomach is heavy, swollen with the fully-formed foetus,
The seeds which came from the father become a burden to the
    mother

Inflicting unbearable pains as the uterus swells.
For when, in the struggle of giving birth, the womb contracts,
The woman alone pays the price, with such great physical
    danger,
For what the two of them created together; perhaps hope
    alleviates the pain,
180 If the son that is born lives; and yet it very often happens
That with her groans she brings forth a dead child.
Often the mother also dies at the same time, providing a
    double tomb
For the child that was not even born at the time of its death.
How often does this slightly less terrible event occur,
That the mother alone dies in childbirth? As she brings forth
    her burden
When the child leaves her, so does her soul. What if the child
Raised and fed for a long time is snatched away by death,
The child viewed as the sole hope, and she loses everything
That her joy promised, all that she was looking forward to?
190 Much more serious than all these things is if envious death by
    chance
Snatches the young child away prematurely, before it has been
    washed
In the heavenly waters, born only for the harsh fate of hell.
Such a child, when he ceases to be the son of his mother
Will be the son of perdition; then the grieving parents regret
Giving birth to this body which they brought forth only for the
    flames.
Who could recount the risks of such a terrible event,
Dangers to which pride in the beloved body is exposed?
But under the law by which you are now bound
Your extensive freedom can offer you a different fate
200 So that the wicked chains of this treacherous world do not bind
    you.
You are following in Mary's footsteps to whom the Almighty
    granted
That she should rejoice in the double crown of virgin and
    mother
When she conceived God in the flesh, and the Creator of
    heaven
Entered the womb through closed doors, unlocking the
    mysteries.

# ARATOR

## Introduction

There is no evidence of any commentary in Latin on the Acts of the Apostles before the verse commentary composed by Arator in 544: although Cassiodorus commissioned a translation into Latin of John Chrysostom's *Homilies on the Acts of the Apostles*, we have no evidence that this work would have been known to Arator. Arator's work was, however, clearly known to Bede who wrote one of the few commentaries on this New Testament book in the early eighth century for Bede pays tribute to Arator in his preface and often quotes from the work.

Although Arator is mentioned by such contemporaries as Cassiodorus and Ennodius, we know neither the date of his birth nor his death. It would seem that the author was a member of the Italian aristocracy who was given a traditional education and who held office at the court of the Ostrogothic kings at Ravenna until forced by the dangers caused by the tension between the Ostrogothic kingdom and Constantinople to flee to Rome and the protection of Pope Vigilius to whom he dedicated his poem known as the *Historia Apostolica* or the *De Actibus Apostolorum* (*The History of the Apostles* or *On the Acts of the Apostles*). By this stage he had abandoned his secular career in favour of service to the Church, becoming a sub-deacon. Part of this service included the composition of the poem in 2336 hexameters which he apparently wrote both to thank Vigilius for his protection and to praise God. He considered using the Psalms or Genesis as the basis for his poem but then decided on Acts because it offered not only the historical account of the apostolic work of Peter and Paul but also contemporary relevance to the Church, centred on Rome, through the figure of St Peter, as well as the possibility of showing, as many other poets of this period strive to do, how the

New Testament provides fulfilment of events in the Old Testament. Once again we find many passages of typological interpretation, here focusing particularly on the theme of baptism, as Hillier has clearly shown: Arator manages not only to emphasize any reference in the scriptural text to baptism, but adds many interpretations which impute a baptismal significance to passages of Acts where there is no obvious reference to such a theme.

Arator's poem was widely read in the Middle Ages, despite the fact that his style does not have the clarity found in the biblical epics of Sedulius or Avitus. Even in the more literal passages (and here, too, Arator often rearranges the order of events or omits sections at will), with which the allegorical passages alternate, Arator favours such oblique expressions that many passages remain obscure. If Sedulius' *Carmen Paschale* was the inspiration behind Arator's decision to provide spiritual interpretations of the literal scriptural account, one can still see evidence of the inspiration offered by Virgil and other pagan poets, as in the description of the storm and shipwreck experienced by St Paul on his way to Rome (Acts 27) which in many aspects resembles the description of the storm that drives Aeneas onto the African shore near Carthage when he is attempting to reach Italy and the site of the future Rome (*Aeneid,* Book 1).

## Text

Latin text: PL 68, CSEL 72 (1951).

Example of Latin verse form; hexameters

1.1–7

Ut sceleris Iudaea sui polluta cruore,
Ausa nefas, complevit opus rerumque creator
Hoc quod ab humanis sumpsit sine semine membris
Humana pro stirpe dedit, dignatus ut ima
Tangeret inferni, non linquens ardua caeli,
Solvit ab aeterna damnatas nocte tenebras
Ad Manes ingressa dies.

## Historia Apostolica 1.1007–1076

*Peter's release from prison*

*Based on Acts 12:1–17*

    Peter is shut up in the dark prison, but not without light,
    And the darkness with its dim gloom cannot
    Blot out the bright light of the Church. That fear causes
1010 The torture to be shared by all; Peter's imprisonment
    Was a public penalty. But the shepherd rules over his own
        sheepfold,
    When the guardian is safe, he who is enriched with honour
    By the love which confessed the Lord three times. Peter takes
        his name
    From the word 'rock' and carries the words for ever,
    Supporting foundations which will never be allowed to collapse.
    Awaited by your people and dear to them for all time,
    Come to us now, Peter. Go out to all of them who are
    Now roused by your earlier concern. Now in the depths of night
    A shining white angel bearing stars enters the prison,
1020 Accompanied by bright daylight; at the arrival of the heavenly
        messenger
    The shadows of the prison flee; darkness is put to flight and
        vanishes;
    A new morning star shines forth; the blackness is banished,
    The gloom of dusk transformed and they look upon the sun.
    While a troop of soldiers guarded him, Peter's body slept
    Even while he was in chains, but meanwhile faith which never
        sleeps
    Remained awake in him; as the Song of Songs proclaims:
    'I sleep but my heart is awake.'[1] Learn with joy the lesson
    Of this figure, you who have deserved to be reborn in the clear
        spring
    And perceive with loving heart the image prefigured
1030 In Peter's sacred body: the angel himself points out
    This path lying open to virtue; touching Peter's side he strikes
    That part where the Church has its origin; the messenger
        raised him from where
    He knew the Church had sprung. To the side of the ark
    Noah added sacred doors when the animals were shut inside;
        through these came

Salvation when the flood caused devastation. Eve was brought forth
From her husband as he slept, a shoot springing from his side,
Given a name meaning 'life'; she would have remained like this longer
If she had never sinned; afterwards Christ, the mystic Adam,
Deigned to give his body up to the cross, and in the destruction of the flesh
1040 To be oppressed by death so that life might return, consecrating
The new gift of liquid as it poured from his side;[2] now the angel
Calls Peter through that part of his body, so that every mind may believe
That the glory of the Church stands firm in him and may hold fast to the faith
With his heavenly deliverer; it was on the angel's orders that these feet
Were granted sandals, the feet touched by the Master's right hand
That had cleansed him completely in the waters. As they set forth
The closed gates opened for them; he thinks everything
That happens is a trick of sleep, but the divine majesty
That knows no trickery has prepared true rewards for him.
1050 Now the iron gate to the prison opens: the stiff gates relax their bolts.
Rejecting the intensity of the gentiles' harsh savagery
He tames all that is savage, so that the fixed door might not prevent
The world's journey from taking its future course: say, universal glory,
Why is it surprising if the iron gates give way to Peter?
It was he whom God deputed to guard the halls of heaven,
Granting him the highest position in his church,
And ordered him to conquer hell;[3] then freed from his enemy
He celebrated his divine achievement. It was a young girl who first
Proved that he had returned from darkness, because the grace of Christ
1060 Granted the same thing as when Christ rose again: then he first appeared
To women and the glory of the flesh returning addressed members

Of that female sex to which his mother belonged.[4] It is clear,
    too, that from then on
The Church decided Peter would be its prophet, so that as it
    spread
He might bring its joys to the whole flock. Whose speech
    would be able
To explain such things, whose words could praise their
    importance?
That terrible fear which had affected their icy limbs[5]
Was a measure of their joy; throughout all ages there remains
The crowning dignity of this pledge, shining on like a star,
Consecrated by Peter with his body and by the angel with its
    words.
1070 By these chains our faith is strengthened, by these chains, O
    Rome,
Perpetual salvation is yours; encircled by their grip
You will always be free, for what is not possible for those
    chains
Which he touched, he who can set all things free? By his hand
These things remain unconquered and the city walls
Made sacred by his triumph no enemy will ever shake.
He who opens the gates to the stars has blocked the path to
    war.

# VENANTIUS FORTUNATUS

## Introduction

Venantius Fortunatus was born around 540 in Northern Italy. He studied at Ravenna, but after going on a pilgrimage to the shrine of St Martin at Tours, he settled in Poitiers where he spent the rest of his life until his death some time after 600. As well as becoming Bishop of Poitiers, he also acted as the priest and spiritual adviser for the convent community of the Holy Cross, in which capacity he became a close friend of the abbess Radegund, the ex-queen and daughter-in-law of King Clovis, whose dramatic life formed the subject of one of the seven prose hagiographies composed by him. However, it is as a poet that Fortunatus is most well known, having composed about 300 hymns, elegies, epigrams, epitaphs, panegyrics and works of consolation (collected in eleven books) as well as a verse Life of St Martin in four books of hexameters. His most famous works are probably the hymns that he wrote on the Cross, on the occasion of the presentation of a fragment of the True Cross by the Emperor Justinian to Radegund's convent – especially the two known by their opening words: *Vexilla regis* and *Pange, lingua*. The slightly less familiar *Crux benedicta nitet* is translated below, with which the fifth-century poem *De Ligno Crucis* can be compared, for both poems depict the Lord's cross as a tree bearing life-giving fruit.

His other poems deserve to be better known. Some reveal the poet's particular skill in descriptions of nature as in the long Easter hymn (3.9). Many are polished addresses to distinguished people in the world of ecclesiastical and Merovingian court politics; as Bishop of Poitiers Fortunatus inevitably had dealings not only with those in the monastic community and other churchmen but with the secular leaders. The savage world of Merovingian dynastic politics is well hidden behind Fortunatus' polished verse. Poem 9.2, three excerpts from which are translated here, is addressed to Chilperic and his wife Fredegund on the death of their small sons Dagobert and Chlodobert from dysentery in 580. It is a respectful and sympathetic attempt to console the suffering king and queen which gives little idea of the suffering these two had inflicted on others: Chilperic was engaged in a long civil war against his brothers, he had had his first two wives killed and a few years later he himself was to be assassinated, possibly by Fredegund herself. A darker picture of life in contemporary Gaul and the characters of the Merovingian kings is given by Gregory of Tours in his *History of the Franks* who refers to Chilperic as the Herod and Nero of the time. The consolation, which forms a pair with Poem 9.3, opens with a general lament that death is part of the human condition, inherited from Adam. Fortunatus then offers a catalogue of great men from the Old Testament, all of whom suffered death despite their greatness; indeed, all humans are powerless in the face of death over which God alone has control. The poet provides more personal consolation towards the end of this long poem when he says that Chilperic's sons are privileged to have died and to have reached the joys of heaven early, and expresses his certainty that they will be reunited with their parents at the resurrection.

## Texts

Latin text: PL 88, MGH AA 4 (1881–5).

Example of Latin verse form; elegiac couplets

*Poem 2.1.1–6*

Crux benedicta nitet, dominus qua carne pependit
    Atque cruore suo vulnera nostra lavat,
Mitis amore pio pro nobis victima factus
    Traxit ab ore lupi qua sacer agnus oves,
Transfixis palmis ubi mundum a clade redemit
    Atque suo clausit funere mortis iter.

## Poem 2.1 (The Lord's Cross)

The blessed cross shines bright on which the Lord incarnate
    hung
And with his blood he washes our wounds,

Becoming for us a sacrificial offering, gentle in his devoted
    love:
The holy lamb snatched the sheep from the wolf's maw
When with hands transfixed he redeemed the world from
    disaster,
Blocking death's path by his own death.
Here was that hand pierced by the bloody nails,
The hand that snatched Paul from sin, Peter from death.
O sweet and noble tree, powerful in your fruitfulness,
10  Since you bear such fresh fruits on your branches.
This tree's new fragrance makes the corpses of the dead rise
    up
And those who were deprived of day return to life.
Summer's heat will not burn beneath the leaves of this tree
Neither will the moon by night nor the sun at noon.
Planted beside the rushing waters you shine forth,
Spreading your leafy locks, adorned with fresh blossom.
Between your arms a vine is hung from which
There flow sweet wines, coloured red as blood.

## Poem 9.2 Consolation to Chilperic and Fredegund on the death of their sons 1–10

O harsh condition and irreversible destiny of time,
Allotted to humankind at its tragic beginning
When the seductive serpent spat poison from its fang
And by the serpent's bite Eve in her guilt became death.
From that time our father Adam gave the earth suffering
And from our mother the world, groaning, received a bitter
    gift.
By their transgressions both of them are condemned to
    disgrace:
He is afflicted with toil, she labours in childbearing.
Thence comes devouring death, handed down to their
    descendants,
10  Their baneful origin bringing destruction on their heirs.

## 53–87

And so what are we to do, I ask you now, your excellency,
When we who are guilty can offer no remedy?
We weep, we groan but we can be of no use:

Grief fills our eyes and wealth brings no benefit.
We are tormented deep within, our hearts are rent by sorrow;
Those we love are dead, our eyes cannot see for weeping.
Look how love is called upon, but no lover is now recalled
60  And he who is covered by a sturdy tombstone cannot now
        return to us.
Death is deaf: it shuns us even if we call on it and will not hear;
Hard-hearted it does not know how to respond to pious
        affection.
But I will make that journey with everyone else, whether I like
        it or not;
We will all leave this place and no one returns from there
Until the dead body lives again at the coming of the Lord,
And man rises again from his own dust
When his moist skin begins to cover the dry ashes
And living corpses leap from the tombs.
And so we will all go to inhabit another realm,
70  We who are held in a foreign land will go to our home.
Therefore do not be tormented, good king, most powerful
        prince,
By the fact that your sons are going where every man must go.
The vessel of clay is made in the way the potter wishes
And when the potter wishes the vessels are smashed.
We cannot resist the orders of the Almighty
In whose sight the stars and earth tremble.
He himself creates man: what can we say?
The one who gave also takes back: he is not to be blamed.
Look, we are formed by him and from him our life comes.
80  When he commands, we who are his creation must leave.
If he wishes, he whose works please him, he can change in an
        hour
The mountains, the seas and the stars: what can man do who is
        but smoke?
And so I pray you, mighty king, do what may profit you most,
What may benefit your soul with God's help.
Be strong and dignified, overcome your grief with patience;
A burden that cannot be avoided must be endured.


107–130

And so thanks should instead be given to our God
Who causes those from your seed to go to heaven

167

And chooses the loveliest jewels from the dung of the world,
110 Leading them out of the mud to the stars by his throne.
Your harvest pleased God and he stores it in his barns
When he reaps the sweet grains with the tender ears of corn.
It is not chaff you have begotten – you bring forth whole corn
Which is not to be burnt in the fire but recreated in heaven;
They particularly deserve to be taken hence, purified as they
were
By holy baptism, and renewed in the cleansing stream.
Standing before God like splendid vessels of gold
Or like a beautiful lamp shining on its stand,
Unblemished souls, always radiant with glory,
120 They retain a place in the realm of the living
And planted in the house of the Lord they bloom in the light
Like white lilies set among red roses.
And when the Lord commands the buried limbs to return,
Then your sons will be clothed in lovely robes
And triumphal tunics woven with reddish gold,
And on their brows will be set diadems studded with many
jewels.
A snow-white tunic will cover their white chests
And a bright belt tie up their purple togas.
Then you, their father and mother, will rejoice with them
130 When you see them among the men of heaven.

# GLOSSARY OF
# METRICAL TERMS

The quantitative metres of Greek and Latin Antiquity were determined by the length of each syllable, rather than by word accent, as
was the case with the rhythmic poetry which became popular later in
the development of Latin poetry. Each syllable was considered either
long or short, depending on a number of factors such as the length of
the vowels and the different combinations of vowels and consonants:
diphthongs (double vowels), for example, were regarded as by nature
long, while single vowels might be long or short. Taking the length
of each syllable into account, words were combined into patterns
based on the repetition of certain metrical 'feet' such as the dactyl
(comprising one long and two short syllables), the iamb (a short followed by a long syllable), the trochee (a long followed by a short
syllable) – to name but the most common metrical building blocks.
Later rhythmic poetry often took over the same patterns but based
them on word accent rather than syllable length.

**Asclepiads**:   the basic asclepiad line taken over into Latin poetry
from Greek by Horace comprises three long syllables, two short,
two long, two short and finally a dactyl: Prudentius composes his
preface to the work *Contra Symmachum* in asclepiads, beginning
with the line *Paulus, praeco Dei, qui fera gentium*. In the stanza form
known as the Second Asclepiad, three asclepiadic lines are followed by a glyconic (three long syllables, two short and a dactyl):
this verse form is used by Endelechius for his *Eclogue*.

**(Dactylic) hexameter**:   a line of six feet made up of dactyls (a long
syllable followed by by two short ones) and spondees (two long syllables), as in the opening of Adam's prayer in the *Alethia* of
Claudius Marius Victorius (2.42): *Omnipotens auctor mundi rerumque
creator*.

**Dactylic trimeter hypercatalectic**: this post-classical form is used by Prudentius for the third poem of his *Peristephanon* and the third hymn of the *Cathemerinon*, and by Ausonius for an epitaph and an epigram (X.28, XIX.89, ed. Green). Prudentius uses it in stanzas or verses of five lines. Each line consists of three dactyls followed by one extra syllable. The example is taken from the beginning of Prudentius' third *Cathemerinon* hymn: *O crucifer bone, lucisator*.

**Elegiac couplet**: this consists of a hexameter followed by a pentameter. Venantius Fortunatus composed most of his poetry in elegiac couplets, as for example his poem on Easter (3.9) which begins:

> Tempora florigero rutilant distincta sereno
> Et maiore poli lumine porta patet.

**Iambic dimeter**: each line of this metre is composed of two iambic metra, i.e. eight syllables of alternating short and long syllables. Stanzas made up of lines of iambic dimeters were used by Ambrose in all his hymns and by many later hymn writers. An example of such a line is *Deus creator omnium*.

**Iambic trimeter**: each line of this metre is composed of three iambic metra, i.e. twelve syllables of alternating short and long syllables. This metre is sometimes referred to as the iambic senarius. Alternating iambic trimeters and dimeters was the verse form chosen by Horace for the first ten of his Epodes; it was popular with Ausonius, and is used by his friend Paulinus of Nola in his tenth poem (19-20), addressed to Ausonius:

> Ego te per omne quod datum mortalibus
> Et destinatum saeculum est

In the ninth poem of the *Peristephanon* Prudentius alternates dactylic hexameters with iambic trimeters.

**Pentameter**: a line made up of five dactylic or spondaic feet, with a caesura, or break, after the first syllable of the third foot, as in line 90 of Book 2 of Orientius' *Commonitorium*: *Praemia qui sperat, desidiam fugiat.*

**Sapphics**: this is the form used by Paulinus for his poem 17, a poem of farewell, and by Prudentius in the fourth poem of the *Peristephanon*. The sapphic four-line stanza is formed from three eleven-syllable lines (hendecasyllables) followed by a five-syllable line consisting of an adonius (a dactyl and a trochee or spondee). Prudentius' poem opens thus:

> Bis novem noster populus sub uno
> Martyrum servat cineres sepulchro,
> Caesaraugustam vocitamus urbem,
>     Res cui tanta est.

**Trochaic tetrameter catalectic**   (also known as **trochaic septenarii**): this metre forms a line of fifteen syllables of alternating long and short syllables, with a break usual after the eighth syllable. It was widely used in Roman drama and in marching songs, and was adopted by Venantius Fortunatus for his hymn on the cross (2.2) *Pange, lingua, gloriosi proelium certaminis* and by Prudentius for the first poem of the *Peristephanon* which opens *Scripta sunt caelo duorum martyrum vocabula*. It is also the metre closest to the form of rhythmic verse used by Augustine for his *Psalm against the Donatists*.

# NOTES

## Background to the texts

1 J.L. Vives, *On Education*, E. Watson (trans.) (Cambridge: Cambridge University Press, 1913, p. 159). Vives does, however, admit that these waters, though muddy, are health-giving.

2 Martin Luther in a disputation of 1540 entitled *De divinitate et humanitate Christi.*

3 Colet condemns later Latin writers who have poisoned true Latin speech, producing what he calls 'bloterature' rather than literature: J.H. Lupton, *Life of Dean Colet* (London: G. Bell and Sons, 1909, pp. 279–280).

4 Bolgar (1977, p. 13) speaks of 'an intuitive judgement that the pagan writers of the period before 600 CE had some important characteristic in common which their Christian contemporaries and medieval successors manifestly lacked'.

5 Conrad of Hirsau in the twelfth century discusses the differences between secular poets and the 'ecclesiastici', among whom he includes Sedulius, Prudentius, Juvencus, etc.: he says that in the works of the latter there is a double meaning which gives both the literal truth and a spiritual understanding.

6 Braun (1985).

7 One of the early poets, Commodian, has been assigned to the third century by some critics, while others consider his work to date from the fifth century. If, as some suggest, Commodian came from Africa, it may be that the earlier date is more likely, given that Africa was slightly ahead of Rome in the development of a body of Christian Latin literature. Commodian's two poems, *Carmen Apologeticum* (*Carmen de duobus populis*) and *Instructiones*, are edited by J. Martin in CCSL vol. 128 (1960); the *Instructiones* have been translated in the fourth volume of the series *The Ante-Nicene Fathers* (T. & T. Clark, Edinburgh, repr. 1994: pp. 203–218). A number of poems, such as those on the subject of Sodom and Jonah, have been attributed to Tertullian and Cyprian of Carthage which would place them in the third century but the case for such attributions has not been proved and has generally been regarded with suspicion by modern scholars. These poems have also been translated in the fourth volume of *The Ante-Nicene Fathers*, pp. 127–165.

8 In the Roman province of Africa Latin seems to have been used for the liturgy rather earlier than in Rome, and it is from Africa that some of the great early Latin writers, such as Tertullian, sprang. Moreover, the earliest translation of

the Bible from Greek into Latin may well have been made in North Africa where the Christian communities spoke Latin rather than Greek.

9 Pliny, in a letter to the Emperor Trajan (10.96.7) dating from the early second century, mentions Christians in Bithynia, now part of Turkey, who met regularly before dawn on a fixed day to chant verses antiphonally in honour of Christ as if to a god; such chants or hymns would presumably have been in Greek. In the case of Syriac hymns, it seems they reached their peak during the fourth century with the work of Ephraem the Syrian.

10 J. Fontaine, 'Le poète latin chrétien nouveau psalmiste', in Fontaine (1980, pp. 132–133).

11 Tertullian, *A Treatise on the Soul*, 9.

12 Herzog (1975) in his book on biblical epic rejected the distinction between Christian substance and pagan form.

13 Charlet (1988).

14 On the theory of *Kontrastimitation*, see Thraede (1965).

15 Charlet (1988, p. 85).

16 Augustine puts this view clearly in his discussion of rhetoric in his work, *On Christian Teaching*, 4.12.27.

17 For a convenient summary of Christian attitudes to pagan literature and learning, see Roberts (1985, pp. 62–63).

18 Lactantius, *The Divine Institutes*, preface to Book 1.

19 Paulinus of Nola, *Letter* 16.11 (trans. P.G. Walsh in ACW 35).

20 C. Mohrmann (1955).

21 Jerome, *Letter* 53.10, addressed to Paulinus of Nola.

22 Lactantius, *The Divine Institutes*, 5.1 writes that, 'poets are pernicious because they are easily able to ensnare unwary souls by the sweetness of their discourse and of their poems flowing with delightful modulation. These are sweets that contain poison.'

23 Augustine, *Letter* 26.

24 See for example, Jerome, *Letter* 21.13.

25 Hesiod, *Theogony*, 27–28.

26 Xenophanes (ed. Diels-Kranz, vol. 1. 1) B11 and B1.21-2; cf. Plato, *Republic*, 377d4–6.

27 Aristotle, *Poetics*, 51a36–51b11.

28 Allegory is used already in the New Testament, as for example by Christ at John 3:14 in his interpretation of the brazen serpent of Numbers 21:9 and by St Paul in his interpretation of the story of Abraham and Sarah and Hagar in Galatians 4:22–26.

29 It is true that Virgil's fourth Eclogue was regarded by some as foretelling the coming of the Messiah, see, for example, Augustine, *Letter* 137.3.12 and Courcelle (1957), and that Proba, using lines of Virgil to give an account of salvation history, thinks she can show that Virgil told of the benefits that Christ has brought.

30 Augustine, *City of God*, 2.14.

31 See particularly Plato's discussion in Books 3 and 10 of the *Republic*.

32 See Jerome PL 28.1140.

33 See Augustine, *On Christian Teaching*, 2.40.60 and Jerome, *Letter* 70 for enormously influential advice on a guardedly positive treatment of secular learning, justified by these two Christians in terms of allegorical interpretations of the Old Testament passages telling of the carrying off of the

Egyptian treasures (Exodus 12:35–36) and the treatment of the captive slave girl (Deuteronomy 21:10ff.).

34  Lactantius, *The Divine Institutes*, 6.21.

35  See Augustine, *On Christian Teaching*, 4.6.9ff.

36  See Horace, *Odes*, 3.30.6–8.

37  See Paulinus of Nola, *Poem* 21.

38  Recent German scholars, such as Thraede and Herzog, have tended to reject the division between form and content, but such a view is hard to defend in the face of what the early Christian Latin poets themselves say on the subject.

39  Prudentius, *Hamartigenia*, 159–207; Dracontius, *De Laudibus Dei*, 1.459–491.

40  See P. Brown (1967) Chapter 5 on Augustine's involvement with Manicheism.

41  Brown (1967) Chapter 19.

42  The failure to make a proper distinction between the persons of the Trinity was usually labelled as Sabellian.

43  See Nodes (1984).

44  See Gregory of Tours, *History of the Franks*, 2.34.

45  Nodes (1993, p. 131) writes, 'The reflections on Genesis in the patristic allegorical traditions were concerned with virtually every important doctrinal theme, but the fundamental doctrines of the nature of God and the universe received special attention.' Among such patristic commentaries were the *Hexaemeron* works of Basil in Greek and Ambrose in Latin, and books 11–13 of Augustine's *Confessions* (in which he gave a figurative interpretation of the text in which the creation account is shown to be prophetic of the new creation in Christ), all dating from the second half of the fourth century. Augustine was the only Latin author actually to write commentaries on the early chapters of Genesis in his works *De Genesi ad litteram* (*On the literal interpretation of Genesis*), *De Genesi ad litteram liber imperfectus* (*An unfinished book on the literal interpretation of Genesis*) and the *De Genesi Contra Manichaeos* (*On Genesis against the Manichees*).

46  For a contemporary reference to the suffering caused by the events surrounding the fall of Rome, see Jerome, *Letter* 127.12.

47  Tertullian, *On the Prescription against Heretics*, 7, the same chapter in which he famously rails, 'What has Athens to do with Jerusalem? What concord is there between the Academy and the Church? What between heretics and Christians?'

48  Augustine, *Tractate on the Gospel of John*, 42.10.

49  J.M. Evans (1968), *Paradise Lost and the Genesis Tradition*, Oxford: Clarendon Press.

50  Gregory of Tours, *History of the Franks*, 5.44.

51  Philip Hardie (1993), *The Epic Successors of Virgil*, Cambridge: Cambridge University Press.

52  Jerome, *Letter* 53.7.3.

53  See, for example, the work of Macklin Smith (1976) on Prudentius.

54  See, for example, Augustine *Confessions*, 5.14 for Ambrose's influence on Augustine's view of the Bible as containing a spiritual meaning.

55  Avitus 1.160–169; Augustine, *Tractate on the Gospel of John,* 120.2.

56  Dermot Small (1986, pp. 236–237).

57  Hillier (1993).

58  See H. de Lubac (1998).

59  Michael Roberts (1985), *Biblical Epic and Rhetorical Paraphrase in Late Antiquity*, Liverpool: F. Cairns.

## Lactantius

1 Gregory of Tours, in his work *De Cursu Stellarum* (Chapter 12), attributes the poem to Lactantius, and Alcuin, in his poem about York, mentions Lactantius in his list of Christian poets (line 1552). On the other hand, the earliest extant manuscript of this poem does not give the name of the author.

2 Fitzpatrick (1933, pp. 12–15) summarizes the various versions current in Antiquity.

3 In the First Epistle of Clement of Rome (Chapter 25), the author summarizes the myth which he regards as a sign of the resurrection, and Tertullian, in his work *De resurrectione carnis* (Chapter 13) argues that the case of the phoenix gives us hope that we too will rise again after death. Ambrose in the *Hexaemeron* says that the phoenix teaches us about resurrection (PL 14.238). In early Christian Latin poetry the phoenix is also mentioned by Commodian (*Carmen de duobus populis*, 139–140), Dracontius (1.653), Avitus (1.239) and Venantius Fortunatus (1.15.51ff.).

4 Phaethon, son of the sun god Helios, according to Greek legend, asked to drive his father's chariot across the sky but he was unable to control the horses and so he came close to setting fire to the earth: Zeus had to intervene to save the world. See Ovid, *Metamorphoses*, Book 2.

5 Deucalion was the Greek mythological version of Noah: he and his wife Pyrrha were the sole survivors of the flood sent by Zeus to destroy the world as a punishment for mankind's wickedness. See Ovid, *Metamorphoses*, Book 1.

6 The author is referring to the ostrich.

## Juvencus

1 Jerome, *De Viris Illustribus*, 84; Jerome also mentions Juvencus in his *Letter* 70 and in his commentary on Matthew 2.11.

2 An example of the way he paraphrases can be taken from Book 2 (224–226): the text of John 3:16, 'God so loved the world that he gave his only-begotten son so that everyone who believes in him may not perish but have eternal life' runs as follows in the Latin (Vulgate) version: *Sic enim dilexit Deus mundum ut Filium suum unigenitum daret ut omnis qui credit in eum non pereat sed habeat vitam aeternam.* This, or a similar text derived from the Old Latin version of the Bible, Juvencus transforms into the following 3 hexameter lines: *Namque Deus mundum tanto dilexit amore/ Eius ut in terras descenderet unica proles/ Credentes Domino vitae iunctura perenni.*

3 Only about one-fifth of the verses are based on a Gospel other than that of St Matthew: indeed, Roger Bacon in the thirteenth century writes in his *Compendium studii philosophiae* that Juvencus 'put St Matthew's Gospel into verse'. Juvencus does, however, turn to St Luke for the account of Christ's infancy (though he rearranges the order of events) and to St John for the account of the raising of Lazarus.

4 Cf. Prudentius' prayer at the end of the *Hamartigenia* in which he prays that his soul may avoid the greedy fires of hell.

5 Cf. Micah 5:2.

6 Lines 250–251 are cited by Jerome, *Commentary on Matthew*, 1.2.11 (CCSL 77.13).

7 Cf. Zechariah 13:7.

# Proba

1 Augustine, *Letter* 130 and John Chrysostom, *Letter* 168.
2 See *Patrology* (1986, pp. 271–272) for more information on these cento works.
3 Virgil, *Aeneid*, 8.280.
4 Virgil, *Aeneid*, 1.214.
5 Virgil, *Aeneid*, 1.706.
6 Virgil, *Aeneid*, 1.723.
7 Virgil, *Aeneid*, 2.479.
8 Virgil, *Aeneid*, 5.94.
9 Virgil, *Aeneid*, 12.196.
10 Virgil, *Aeneid*, 1.730; *Aeneid*, 11.241.
11 Virgil, *Aeneid,* 12.173.
12 Virgil, *Georgics*, 2.243.
13 Virgil, *Aeneid*, 1.729.
14 Virgil, *Aeneid*, 12.836.
15 Virgil, *Aeneid*, 10.153.
16 Virgil, *Aeneid*, 3.485.
17 Virgil, *Aeneid*, 3.103.
18 Virgil, *Aeneid*, 5.305.
19 Virgil, *Aeneid*, 5.863.
20 Virgil, *Aeneid*, 5.348.
21 Virgil, *Aeneid*, 5.349.
22 Virgil, *Aeneid*, 8.170.
23 Virgil, *Aeneid*, 5.814.
24 Virgil, *Aeneid*, 8.386.
25 Virgil, *Aeneid*, 7.536.
26 Virgil, *Aeneid*, 5.49.
27 Virgil, *Aeneid*, 1.562.
28 Virgil, *Aeneid*, 4.115.
29 Virgil, *Aeneid*, 10.608.
30 Virgil, *Aeneid*, 5.815.
31 Virgil, *Aeneid*, 10.594.
32 Virgil, *Aeneid*, 3.718.
33 Virgil, *Aeneid*, 8.30.

# Damasus

1 Jerome, *Letter* 22.22.
2 On Agnes, see also Ambrose, *On Virgins*, 1.2; Ambrose, *Hymn* 8 (translated below); Prudentius, *Peristephanon*, 14; Palmer (1989, pp. 250–253).
3 Cf. 1 Corinthians 6:19 for the idea of the body as the temple of the Lord.

# Ambrose

1 Augustine, *Confessions*, 9.6–7 and Paulinus, *Life of Ambrose*, 13.
2 See Ambrose, *Sermo contra Auxentium*, 34, where Ambrose mentions the popularity of his hymns and speaks of them in terms of an expression of faith in the Trinity.

3 Cf. Psalm 80:1–2.
4 This is the verse with which the hymn begins in many modern translated versions: 'Come thou redeemer of the earth'.

## Augustine

1 Augustine, *Retractions*, 1.20.
2 Cf. Prudentius, *Apotheosis*, Preface 41–56.
3 Cf. Matthew 3:12, Luke 3:17.
4 Cf. Matthew 13:24–30, 37–43 for Christ's parables on the seed.
5 Augustine seems to be alluding to the Macarius who, as imperial emissary, was sent to investigate the problems in North Africa in the 340s and who dealt most harshly with the Donatists.
6 Cf. 1 Kings 19:18, Romans 11:4.
7 Cf. 1 Timothy 2:1–2.
8 Psalm 72:10.

## Paulinus of Nola

1 In *Poem* 7 Paulinus uses iambic trimeters in his paraphrase of the first psalm, which despite its biblical content is reminiscent of Horace's second Epode; *Poem 17*, a poem of farewell to his friend Nicetas (who may have been the author of the *Te Deum*) is written in sapphics.
2 This theme comes out in much of Paulinus' work, particularly in lines 1–12 of *Poem 17* to Nicetas.
3 Cf. Witke (1971, pp. 90–4).
4 Celsus had also been the name of Paulinus' own son who died in infancy.
5 Cf. Virgil, *Eclogues*, 1.26.
6 Cf. Virgil, *Georgics*, 3.338.
7 Here Paulinus is describing the nightingale and its song.
8 Cf. 2 Corinthians 4:18.
9 Cf. Matthew 11:30.
10 Cf. Ambrose, *De Excidio Fratris Satyri*, 2.54 and Tertullian, *De resurrectione carnis*, 52 for the same example in support of the idea of resurrection. In general this passage has much in common with Dracontius, *De Laudibus Dei*, 1.623–682.
11 Cf. Virgil, *Georgics*, 1.299.

## Endelechius

1 Cf. Ambrose, *Commentary on Luke*, 10.10 where there is mention of a cattle pest in 386.

## Prudentius

1 Compare the similar format of Sedulius' abecedarian hymn *A solis ortus cardine*, covering Christ's life from birth to resurrection in 23 Ambrosian stanzas; and the even more summary account of Christ's life, focusing on his

death, in Venantius Fortunatus' hymn *Pange lingua gloriosi proelium certaminis*.

2  Cf. *Contra Symmachum* 2.470ff. on the problems of a fatalistic world-view.

3  See Symmachus, *Relatio*, 3 and Ambrose, *Letter* 17 and 18.

4  See pp. 33–45 of the introduction to volume 3 of the Budé edition (ed. Lavarenne) for a list of literary and artistic works in which the influence of Prudentius' poem can be seen.

5  Cf. Genesis 1:31.

6  Prudentius is referring to David as author of the Psalms.

7  The miracle at the wedding at Cana is recorded in John 2:1–10.

8  Matthew 8:3, Mark 1:40, Luke 5:12.

9  John 9:6.

10  Matthew 8:23–26, Mark 4:36–37, Luke 8:22–24.

11  Matthew 9:20–22, Mark 5:25–29, Luke 8:43–44.

12  The story of the widow of Nain and her son is told in Luke 7:11–17.

13  John 11:1–44.

14  Matthew 14:25, Mark 6:48, John 6:19.

15  Luke 8:27–28.

16  Luke 8:30–33.

17  Matthew 14:15–21; Luke 9:10–17.

18  These two lines are echoed by Venantius Fortunatus in his hymn *Pange lingua gloriosi proelium certaminis*.

19  Joshua 7:20–26.

20  The following lines are inspired by Matthew 6:25–34.

21  Prudentius is alluding to the light that went before Moses and the Israelites escaping from Egypt: Exodus 13:21. When Eulalia is said to be fleeing from Egypt it is to be understood in an allegorical sense – she is fleeing from wickedness and persecution in the same way as the Israelites had done.

22  Maximian was emperor in the early years of the fourth century and was instrumental in carrying out persecutions of Christians, as was his fellow emperor Diocletian. The mention of his name may point to a possible date of 303 for Eulalia's martyrdom.

23  The *ungula* was an instrument of torture.

## Cyprian the Poet

1  See *Patrology*: 312–313 for the question of the attribution of these poems. It has been suggested that this Cyprian may also be the author of the biblical prose Cento known as the *Cena Cypriani* (PL 4).

2  See Evans (1968).

3  Nodes (1993, pp. 26–36).

4  Genesis 1:26.

5  Genesis 2:7.

6  Genesis 2:18.

7  Genesis 2:21.

8  Genesis 3:20.

9  Genesis 2:2–3.

10  Genesis 2:19–20.

11  Genesis 1:28–29.

12  Genesis 2:8-9.

13 Genesis 2:10–14.
14 Genesis 2:15–16.
15 The rest of the passage follows the order of the third chapter of Genesis.

## Sedulius

1 Sedulius pours scorn on Arius (who had died some one hundred years earlier) at 1.300 and 322.
2 Psalm 29:3.
3 Cf. Matthew 23:27–28.
4 The CSEL text omits verse 176.
5 Cf. Jerome, *Commentary on Matthew*, 4.27.34 (CCSL 77.271).
6 Allusion to Trinitarian doctrine of one God in three persons.
7 The word schism literally means tearing.
8 Christ refers to himself as the vine at John 15:1.
9 Sedulius is alluding to the parable of the lost sheep, told at Matthew 18:12–14.

## Prosper of Aquitaine

1 Cf. Isaiah 40:6–8.
2 Cf. Christ's words at John 15:4–6.

## Claudius Marius Victorius

1 Sodom is also the subject of the poem of that name mentioned in connection with the *De Ligno Crucis*.
2 This manuscript also contains an early fourth-century anonymous poem of 148 hexameters entitled the *Laudes Domini* (edited by Arevalo in PL 19.379–386) giving an account in Virgilian style of a miracle involving the corpses of a husband and wife which had apparently taken place near Autun in France.
3 See Manitius (1891, p. 180).
4 See especially lines 55–58 and 69–70 of the Prayer for the poet's emphasis on free-will.
5 Cf. Juvenal 10.2ff.
6 Genesis 3:9.

## Paulinus of Pella

1 The same word is used as the title (*Eucharisticum de vita sua*) for a short piece of prose autobiography written by Ennodius, Bishop of Pavia, in the early sixth century; see CSEL 6.393–401. Ennodius was also the author of hymns, poems and epigrams.
2 The sufferings caused by the barbarian invasions are referred to also by Orientius and by the author of the *Carmen de Providentia Divina*.

## De Ligno Crucis

1 This is also the title given to a meditation on the life of Christ by the thir-teenth-century Bonaventure which is regarded as a classic of Franciscan spirituality. In the prologue to this work Bonaventure describes the cross in similar terms to those found in the *De Ligno Crucis* translated here. Compare also Commodian's poem *Instructiones* (Book 1, section 35) entitled 'De Ligno vitae et mortis' (The tree of life and death) in which the poet plays on the connection between the tree of knowledge which brought death to Adam, and the cross of Christ which is a life-giving tree.

2 Isaiah 11:1.

## Orientius

1 The poet names himself at 2.417 of his poem.

## Dracontius

1 These heroes and heroines are also mentioned by Augustine in his work *The City of God* (5.12ff.).

2 For example Dracontius bases his brief description of paradise at the end of the work (3.752–754) on Virgil's description of Elysium in *Aeneid*, 6.638–639.

3 Here Dracontius affirms the unity of the three persons of the Trinity; in Book 2.67–69 he affirms the consubstantiality of the Father and the Son.

4 Cf. Genesis 1:28.

5 For this passage on the certainty of resurrection, cf. Tertullian, *Apologia*, 48:8–9, *De resurrectione carnis*, 12; Minucius Felix 34:11–12, Ambrose, *Hexaemeron*, 5.23.78, Prudentius, *Contra Symmachum,* 2.195–211.

6 Cf. Psalm 51:16–17.

## Avitus

1 Avitus chooses to deal with Genesis 1–3:24, Genesis 6–9:17 and Exodus 1–15:1.

2 For example, Romans 5:15–17.

3 Cf. Virgil, *Aeneid*, 1.279.

4 Ovid, *Tristia*, 4.6.7, Catullus, *Poem,* 64.48.

5 Virgil, *Georgics*, 2.149.

6 The phoenix; cf. Ovid, *Amores*, 2.6.54.

7 Compare Milton, *Paradise Lost*, 5.859–863 for Satan's claim that he created himself.

8 Cf. Virgil, *Aeneid,* 11.407, Juvenal 8.141.

9 Avitus is referring to Eve's son Abel: Genesis 4:8.

## Arator

1 Song of Songs 5:2.

2 Augustine in his *Tractate on the Gospel of John* 120, on John 19:34, mentions

the door in Noah's ark, Eve taken from Adam's side, and Christ as the second Adam in connection with the blood and water that poured from Christ's side on the cross. For further examples of this collection of types, see Hillier (1993) *ad loc.*

3 Lines 1054–1057 are quoted by Bede in his *Exposition on the Acts of the Apostles* (CSEL 121.59)
4 Mark 16:1–8.
5 Cf. Mark 16:8.

# SELECT BIBLIOGRAPHY

*For a fuller bibliography see, for example, those provided by Roberts (1985), Palmer (1989), Evenepoel (1993) and Trout (1999).*

## General works

Bolgar, R.R. (1954, repr. 1977) *The Classical Heritage and its Beneficiaries*, Cambridge: Cambridge University Press.

Braun, R. (1985) 'L'influence de la Bible sur la langue latine tardive', in J. Fontaine and C. Pietri (eds) *Le Monde latin antique et la Bible*, Paris: Beauchesne, pp. 129–142.

Brown, P. (1967) *Augustine of Hippo: A Biography*, London: Faber and Faber Ltd.

Brown, P. (1981) *The Cult of the Saints*, Chicago: University of Chicago Press.

Calder, D.G. and Allen, M. (eds) (1976) *Sources and Analogues of Old English Poetry*, Cambridge: D.S. Brewer.

Charlet, J.-L. (1988) 'Aesthetic trends in Late Latin poetry', *Philologus* 132: 74–85.

*Christianisme et formes littéraires de l'antiquité tardive en occident* (1976) A. Cameron and M. Fuhrmann (eds), Fondation Hardt 23.

Courcelle, P. (1957) 'Les exégèses chrétiennes de la quatrième Églogue', *Revue des études anciennes* 59: 294–319.

*Early Christian Poetry* (1993) J. den Boeft and A. Hilhorst (eds), Leiden: E.J. Brill.

Evans, J.M. (1968) *Paradise Lost and the Genesis Tradition*, Oxford: Clarendon Press.

Evenepoel, W. (1993) 'The place of poetry in Latin Christianity', in *Early Christian Poetry*, J. den Boeft and A. Hilhorst (eds), Leiden: E.J. Brill.

Fontaine, J. (1974) 'L'apport de la tradition poétique romaine à la formation de l'hymnodie latine chrétienne', *Revue des études latines* 52: 318–355.

Fontaine, J. (1980) *Études sur la poésie latine tardive d'Ausone à Prudence*, Paris: Belles Lettres.

Fontaine, J. (1981) *Naissance de la Poésie dans l'Occident chrétien*, Paris: Études Augustiniennes.

Gill, C. and Wiseman, T.P. (eds) (1993) *Lies and Fiction in the Ancient World*, Exeter: University of Exeter Press.

Glauche, G. (1970) *Schullektüre im Mittelalter*, Munich: Arbeo-Gesellschaft.

Hagendahl, H. (1983) *Von Tertullian zu Cassiodor. Die profane literarische Tradition in dem lateinischen christlichen Schrifttum*, Göteborg, Acta Universitatis Gothoburgensis.

Hardie, P. (1993) *The Epic Successors of Virgil*, Cambridge: Cambridge University Press.

Harrison, C. (2000) 'The Rhetoric of Scripture and Preaching', in R. Dodaro and G. Lawless (eds) *Augustine and his critics: Essays in honour of Gerald Bonner*, London/New York: Routledge, pp. 214–230.

Herzog, R. (1975) *Die Bibelepik der lateinischen Spätantike: Formgeschichte einer erbaulichen Gattung*, Munich: Fink Verlag.

Kartschoke, D. (1975) *Bibeldichtung: Studien zur Geschichte der epischen Bibelparaphrase von Juvencus bis Otfried von Weissenburg*, Munich: Fink Verlag.

Kennedy, G. (1989) 'Christianity and criticism', in *The Cambridge History of Literary Criticism*, vol. 1, Cambridge: Cambridge University Press.

Klopsch, P. (1972) *Einführung in die Mittellateinischen Verslehre*, Darmstadt: Wissenschaftliche Buchgesellschaft.

Klopsch, P. (1980) *Einführung in die Dichtungslehren des lateinischen Mittelalters*, Darmstadt: Wissenschaftliche Buchgesellschaft.

Lubac, H. de (1998) *Medieval Exegesis*, vol. 1, Edinburgh: T. & T. Clark.

Manitius, M. (1891) *Geschichte der christlich-lateinischen Poesie bis zur Mitte des 8. Jahrhunderts*, Stuttgart: J.G. Cotta.

Mohrmann, C. (1947) 'La langue et le style de la poésie chrétienne', *Études sur le latin des chrétiens* I.151–168 (= Revue des études latines 25: 280–297).

Mohrmann, C. (1955) 'Problèmes stylistiques dans la littérature latine chrétienne', *Vigiliae Christianae* 9: 222–246.

Nodes, D. (1993) *Doctrine and Exegesis in Biblical Latin Poetry*, Liverpool: F. Cairns.

Norberg, D. (1958) *Introduction à l'étude de la versification latine médiévale*, Stockholm: Almqvist and Wiksell.

*Patrology: The Golden Age of Latin Patristic Literature* (1986) A. di Berardino (ed.), Westminster, MD.

Raby, F.J.E. (1953) *A History of Christian Latin Poetry*, Oxford: Clarendon Press.

Roberts, M. (1985) *Biblical Epic and Rhetorical Paraphrase in Late Antiquity*, Liverpool: F. Cairns.

Roberts, M. (1989) *The Jeweled Style*, Ithaca, NY: Cornell University Press.

Schetter, W. and Gnilka, C. (eds) (1975) *Studien zur Literatur der Spätantike*, Bonn: Habelt.

Thraede, K. (1965) *Studien zur Sprache und Stil des Prudentius*, Göttingen, Hypomnemata 13.

Witke, C. (1971) *Numen Litterarum. The Old and the New in Latin Poetry from Constantine to Gregory*, Leiden: E.J. Brill.

## Works on specific authors

### Ambrose

Fontaine, J. (1992) *Ambroise de Milan: Hymnes*, Paris: Cerf.

### Arator

Hillier, R. (1993) *Arator on the Acts of the Apostles: A Baptismal commentary*, Oxford: Clarendon Press.

### Avitus

Hecquet-Noti, N. (ed.) (1999) *Avit de Vienne: Histoire Spirituelle*, SC 444, Paris: Cerf.
Nodes, D.J. (1984) 'Avitus of Vienne's *Spiritual History* and the Semipelagian controversy: the doctrinal implications of Books 1–3', *Vigiliae Christianae* 38: 185–195.
Shea, G.W. (1997) *The Poems of Alcimus Ecdicius Avitus*, Arizona: Medieval and Renaissance Texts and Studies.

### Claudius Marius Victorius

Nodes, D.J. (1988) 'The seventh day of creation in *Alethia* of Claudius Marius Victor', *Vigiliae Christianae* 42: 59–74.

### *De Ligno Crucis*

Schwind, J. (1989) 'Das pseudocyprianische *Carmen de Pascha seu de Ligno Crucis* in H.-W. Stork (ed.) *Ars et Ecclesia. Festschrift für Franz J. Ronig*, Trier: Paulinus-Verlag.

### Dracontius

Nodes, D.J. (1989) 'Benevolent winds and the Spirit of God in *De laudibus Dei* of Dracontius', *Vigiliae Christianae* 43: 282–292.

### Lactantius

Fitzpatrick, M.C. (1933) *Lactanti De Ave Phoenice*, Philadelphia.

### Paulinus of Nola

Greene, R.P.H. (1971) *The Poetry of Paulinus of Nola*, Brussels: Latomus.
Kohlwes, K. (1979) *Christliche Dichtung und stilistische Form bei Paulinus von Nola*, Bonn: Habelt.
Trout, D. E. (1999) *Paulinus of Nola: Life, Letters and Poems*, Berkeley, CA: University of California Press.

Walsh, P.G. (trans.) (1975) *The Poems of Paulinus of Nola*, ACW 40, New York: Newman Press.

## Paulinus of Pella

Moussy, C. (ed.) *Paulin de Pelle: Poème d'action de graces et prière*, SC 209, Paris: Cerf.

## Proba

Clark, E.A. and Hatch, D. (1981) *The Golden Bough, The Oaken Cross: The Virgilian Cento of Faltonia Betitia Proba*, Ann Arbor, MI: University of Michigan Press.

## Prudentius

Bastiaensen, A.R. (1993) 'Prudentius in recent literary criticism', in *Early Christian Poetry*, J. den Boeft and A. Hillhorst (eds), Leiden: E.J. Brill.

Charlet, J.-L. (1983) 'Prudence et la Bible', *Recherches Augustiniennes* 18: 3–149.

Palmer, A.M. (1989) *Prudentius on the Martyrs*, Oxford: Clarendon Press.

Roberts, M. (1993) *Poetry and the Cult of the Martyrs: The Liber Peristephanon of Prudentius*, Ann Arbor, MI: University of Michigan.

Slavitt, D. (trans.) (1996) *Hymns of Prudentius: The Cathemerinon*, Baltimore: Johns Hopkins University Press.

Smith, M. (1976) *Prudentius' Psychomachia: A Re-examination*, Princeton, NJ: Princeton University Press.

Thraede, K. (1965) *Studien zur Sprache und Stil des Prudentius*, Göttingen, Hypomnemata 13.

## Sedulius

Dermot Small, C. (1986) 'Rhetoric and exegesis in Sedulius' *Carmen Paschale*', *Classica et Medievalia* 37: 223–244.

Springer, C. (1988) *Sedulius' Paschale Carmen: The Gospel as Epic in Late Antiquity*, Leiden: E.J. Brill.

Van der Laan, P.W.A. (1993) 'Le *Carmen Paschale* de Sédulius', in *Early Christian Poetry*, J. den Boeft and A. Hilhorst (eds), Leiden: E.J. Brill.

## Venantius Fortunatus

George, J. (1995) *Personal and Political Poems*, Liverpool: Liverpool University Press.

# INDEX OF NAMES AND SUBJECTS

# INDEX OF BIBLICAL
# REFERENCES

# INDEX OF LITERARY WORKS

193